LOOKING TOWARD ETERNITY

A Life Hereafter?

*Keep smiling Kathryn
God loves you.
Herschel Hill*

LOOKING TOWARD ETERNITY

A Life Hereafter?

HERSCHEL HILL

© 2005 by Herschel Hill. All rights reserved.

Pleasant Word (a division of WinePress Publishing, PO Box 428, Enumclaw, WA 98022) functions only as book publisher. As such, the ultimate design, content, editorial accuracy, and views expressed or implied in this work are those of the author.

No part of this publication may be reproduced, stored in a retrieval system or transmitted in any way by any means—electronic, mechanical, photocopy, recording or otherwise—without the prior permission of the copyright holder, except as provided by USA copyright law.

Unless otherwise noted, all Scriptures are taken from the Holy Bible, New International Version, Copyright © 1973, 1978, 1984 by the International Bible Society. Used by permission of Zondervan Publishing House. The "NIV" and "New International Version" trademarks are registered in the United States Patent and Trademark Office by International Bible Society.

Scripture references marked KJV are taken from the King James Version of the Bible.

ISBN 1-4141-0450-2
Library of Congress Catalog Card Number: 2005925621

TABLE OF CONTENTS

Acknowledgments vii

Chapter 1: Questions About Eternity 9
Chapter 2: A Life Hereafter? 17
Chapter 3: Heaven 21
Chapter 4: Hell 27
Chapter 5: End-Time Judgments 31
Chapter 6: Degrees of Heaven and Hell 47
Chapter 7: Between Physical Death and
    the End of This Age 57
Chapter 8: Resurrection of the Body 65
Chapter 9: Christ, Between the Cross
    and the Resurrection 75
Chapter 10: The Big Picture 87
Chapter 11: Our Final Destination 95

Acknowledgments

This book is dedicated to my precious wife of fifty-one years, Dorothy, who succumbed to lung cancer in 2004. She lovingly encouraged me and supported me throughout the lengthy process of writing these pages. Her gallant battle against a stroke, and then cancer, was a great inspiration for me as I planned and organized my first book, identified and studied related Bible passages, and then penned the words written herein. I know she is now experiencing the peace, joy, and bliss described in the pages of this book.

Also, I want to express my gratitude to the members of my Bible study classes over the last fifteen years. They challenged me with their many questions about the nature of a life after this mortal life. Their questions and their diverse beliefs about that issue prompted me to delve into the Bible to determine what it actually has to say about a life hereafter.

Most of all, I am thankful for the Holy Spirit whose guidance and revelations enabled me to gain a greater understanding of things to come after this life. My prayer is that the results of my Bible study, as presented in this book, are true interpretations of the Bible passages utilized.

Chapter 1

QUESTIONS ABOUT ETERNITY

All of us realize we have a limited time on this earth, that we must face physical death. That is not a pleasant realization, but it is something we cannot avoid. I am sure most of us have wondered at one time or another what is in store for us after this mortal life. Is physical death the end for us, or do we have something to look forward to beyond this life? Most of the world's religions have addressed this question, but the answers they provide are far from uniform. Even devout Christians cling to diverse views regarding the reality and nature of a life hereafter. The Bible, God's Holy Word, contains many references to Heaven, Hell, eternal life, end-time judgments, rewards and crowns, eternal punishment, and resurrection, all associated with a life hereafter. In this book, I address and define each of those places, events, and things as we seek a better understanding of a life after this mortal life.

I have taught adult Bible study classes for over fifteen years, and on numerous occassions my classes addressed the issue of

Looking Toward Eternity: A Life Hereafter?

a life beyond this life. I am always amazed at the wide variety of beliefs held by sincere and dedicated Christians concerning a life hereafter. Their perceptions of Heaven, Hell, end-time judgments, rewards, eternal punishment, and resurrection are vastly different, but each person's view is supposedly based on that individual's interpretation of the Bible. How can it be that so many of us can read the same Bible passages and end up with such different perceptions and interpretations? Perhaps it is because we tend to be influenced so much by tradition, either that of our family or that of our church. We are taught the meaning of a life hereafter in a family setting and/or in church, and we quite often adopt a view very close to the one we have been taught. That view may or may not be based on sound interpretation of the Bible.

My concern about the widespread disagreement pertaining to such a basic area of Christian faith prompted me to delve into God's Word to determine what the Bible actually has to say about a life hereafter. The results of my systematic and comprehensive study of this issue are presented in this book, so join me as we step through that study and review my conclusions. My personal interpretations of individual Bible passages are incorporated into this study, and they are for the most part consistent with those of other Bible commentaries and related publications concerning this issue. The key difference is that my study, unlike other similar studies, does not incorporate those complex and somewhat controversial Bible passages found in books of the Bible such as Daniel in the Old Testament and Revelation in the New Testament. Instead, easy-to-understand passages are utilized, and the interpretations and conclusions presented are such that even the novice Bible student can follow and comprehend them. I have linked all the related Bible passages together in such a way as to give a more straightforward and uncomplicated view of what a life hereafter involves.

Questions About Eternity

This book is written in lay terms, so a very broad spectrum of readers can comprehend the interpretations and conclusions presented herein. My objective in this book is twofold. First, it is my desire that the readers gain a better knowledge and understanding of what the Bible, or Scripture, has to say about a life after this life. Second, it is my goal to motivate and encourage the readers to study the Bible in order to determine for themselves what the Bible teaches about this important matter. The study presented in this book will facilitate a fundamental understanding of what eternity and a life hereafter involve, but the more serious Bible student may be led to study this issue in greater depth to obtain answers to questions not addressed in this study. This book is written for Christians and non-Christians alike.

The Scripture passages utilized in this study are from either the New International Version (NIV) or the King James Version (KJV) of the Bible. The truth and authority of the quoted Bible passages are without question, but the views, conclusions, and comments included herein represent the writer's interpretation and understanding of the Scriptures. You, the reader, most likely disagree with a number of the views and interpretations expressed by the author, and you assuredly have differences of opinion with other readers on some issues. When we have such a question or disagreement about the meaning or application of a particular Bible passage, we turn to other passages for clarification. We let Scripture interpret Scripture. Many passages in the Bible are very difficult to comprehend without turning to other passages dealing with the same issues. Oftentimes, the context or application of an individual Scripture passage is not apparent until other passages are studied and compared to it. I believe this approach to Bible study facilitates a more complete and a clearer understanding of the basic truths presented in the Scriptures.

This study addresses a number of questions and concerns regarding a life hereafter. Our first order of business is to ascertain from the Bible the reality of a life beyond this life. Each of us must face physical death, but what is in store for us after that? The Bible incorporates many passages that address that issue, such as:

> "Then they will go away to eternal punishment, but the righteous to eternal life."
> —Matthew 25:46 NIV

This and related Bible passages are examined in great depth to determine what "eternal life" and "eternal punishment" really mean.

Our second task is to determine the reality and nature of both Heaven and Hell. Are Heaven and Hell real places, and if so, what are they like and who will go there?

> And I heard a great voice out of Heaven saying, Behold, the tabernacle of God is with men, and he will dwell with them, and they shall be his people, and God himself shall be with them, and be their God.
> —Revelation 21:3 KJV

> They will be punished with everlasting destruction and shut out from the presence of the Lord and from the majesty of his power....
> —2 Thessalonians 1:9 NIV

The Bible makes numerous references to Heaven, a place of joy and bliss, and to "everlasting destruction," a place we call Hell. In our study, we examine and interpret a number of Bible passages that address the reality and nature of both Heaven and Hell.

Our third concern is the Second Coming of Christ and subsequent end-time judgments. Will Jesus Christ actually return to earth, and if so, what events will transpire at His second coming? Also, what judgments will take place after Christ returns, and who will be judged? These questions are addressed as we study pertinent Bible passages.

> Therefore judge nothing before the appointed time; wait till the Lord comes. He will bring to light what is hidden in darkness and will expose the motives of men's hearts. At that time each will receive his praise from God.
> —1 Corinthians 4:5 NIV

> For we must all appear before the judgment seat of Christ; that everyone may receive the things done in his body, according to that he hath done, whether it be good or bad.
> —2 Corinthians 5:10 KJV

> Then I saw a great white throne and him who was seated on it. Earth and sky fled from his presence, and there was no place for them. And I saw the dead, great and small, standing before the throne, and books were opened. Another book was opened, which is the book of life. The dead were judged according to what they had done as recorded in the books.
> —Revelation 20:11-12 NIV

These Bible verses and others relate to the Second Coming of Christ, the Judgment Seat of Christ, and the Great White Throne Judgment. We will consider the nature and significance of these future events, for both Christians and non-Christians.

Our fourth task is to determine if there are, or will be, degrees of Heaven and degrees of Hell. We find that there are only two basic classes of people, those who will be assigned to Heaven and those who will be relegated to Hell. But, is Heaven the same for all those who go there, or are there varying degrees of Heaven for its residents? In a like manner, do we find varying degrees of punishment for those relegated to Hell? Also, what is the significance of crowns and rewards in Heaven and punishment in Hell?

Looking Toward Eternity: A Life Hereafter?

> And when the Chief Shepherd appears, you will receive the crown of glory that will never fade away.
> —1 Peter 5:4 NIV

> For the Son of man shall come in the glory of his Father with his angels; and then he shall reward every man according to his works.
> —Matthew 16:27 KJV

> His work will be shown for what it is, because the Day will bring it to light. It will be revealed with fire, and the fire will test the quality of each man's work. If what he has built survives, he will receive his reward. If it is burned up, he will suffer loss; he himself will be saved, but only as one escaping through the flames.
> —1 Corinthians 3:13-15 NIV

> And I saw the dead, small and great, stand before God; and the books were opened: and another book was opened, which is the book of life: and the dead were judged out of those things which were written in the books, according to their works.
> —Revelation 20:12 KJV

In our study, we examine key Bible passages to determine if there indeed is, or will be, different degrees of Heaven and Hell.

Our fifth question has to do with what will happen to us between the times of our physical deaths and the end of this age. If Heaven and Hell are real places, when do they start, or when do we go to one or the other? In essence, what will happen to us between the times of our mortal deaths and the Second Coming of Christ?

> And he said unto Jesus, Lord, remember me when thou comest into thy kingdom. And Jesus said unto him, Verily I say unto thee, To day shalt thou be with me in paradise.
> —Luke 23:42-43 KJV

> For the Lord himself will come down from Heaven, with a loud command, with the voice of the archangel and with the trumpet call of God, and the dead in Christ will rise first. After that, we who are still alive and are left will be caught up together with them in the clouds to meet the Lord in the air. And so we will be with the Lord forever.
> —1 Thessalonians 4:16–17 NIV

> And I saw the dead, small and great, stand before God; and the books were opened: and another book was opened, which is the book of life: and the dead were judged out of those things which were written in the books, according to their works....And whosoever was not found written in the book of life was cast into the lake of fire.
> —Revelation 20:12, 15 KJV

As a significant part of our overall study, we consider and define the place called "Paradise," and we examine pertinent Scripture passages to find out just when we will be relegated to either Heaven or Hell. Perhaps that will help us answer our question about what will happen to us between the times of our physical deaths and Christ's second coming.

Sixth, we address the reality and true meaning of bodily resurrection. The Bible speaks often of a resurrection, but does it refer to bodily resurrection or to resurrection of the soul only? And, if bodily resurrection, what does it involve?

> 'The Son of Man must be delivered into the hands of sinful men, be crucified and on the third day be raised again.'
> —Luke 24:7 NIV

> For since by man came death, by man came also the resurrection of the dead.
> —1 Corinthians 15:21 KJV

Looking Toward Eternity: A Life Hereafter?

> And have hope toward God, which they themselves also allow, that there shall be a resurrection of the dead, both of the just and unjust.
> —Acts 24:15 KJV

We first affirm the bodily resurrection of Jesus Christ and then we determine if each of us will experience a similar bodily resurrection. Included in our analysis are those fortunate people going to Heaven as well as those unfortunate ones going to Hell.

Our seventh question deals with the activity of Jesus between the time of His death on the cross and the time of His resurrection three days later. We examine key Bible passages to determine why Jesus had to die on the cross and what He accomplished in doing so. That gives us clues regarding His activity between His death and His resurrection.

Our eighth concern is our most critical one, that of our final destination. That is a personal matter for each of us, one that no other person can take care of for us. One verse in the Bible sums it up nicely.

> For God so loved the world, that he gave his only begotten Son, that whosoever believeth in him should not perish, but have everlasting life.
> —John 3:16 KJV

We study this verse closely to determine precisely what it means, especially the meaning of "believeth." Our understanding of this verse of Scripture, together with our personal response to it, determines where we will spend eternity. It will be either Heaven or Hell; there is no other final destination available to us.

Chapter  2

A Life Hereafter?

What will happen to each of us after this mortal life, after we die a physical death? Will that be the end for us, or will we have a life hereafter? That is a question that humankind has pondered down through the ages, from the most primitive civilization to the complex society we live in today. Literally hundreds of our world's religions have addressed this most basic question of a life after this life, and they have developed many different views regarding a life hereafter. Even in contemporary religions, there is a variety of beliefs about the reality and nature of a life beyond this mortal life.

No attempt is made in this book to examine and compare the diverse views of the various religions concerning this controversial issue. This study focuses exclusively on the Judeo-Christian perspective of a life hereafter. To do so, we must make some very basic and well-accepted assumptions, none of which have to be proven true. We must accept them on faith.

1. God created everything that exists, including the world and universe in which we live. However, God has always existed; He is eternal.
2. God also sustains and controls His creation. He is active in, and in control of, His creation. God guides and controls history.
3. There is only one true God; all other proclaimed gods are false. Our Creator God is all-powerful, all-knowing, all-loving, omnipresent, and unchanging.
4. The human mind cannot fully comprehend God, but He has revealed Himself to us as God the Father, as God the Son, and as God the Holy Spirit.
5. God sent His Incarnate Son, Jesus Christ, born of the Virgin Mary, to dwell among us and to redeem all of humankind. Through Jesus the Son, we see the character and nature of God the Father.
6. Through God the Holy Spirit, God inspired mere human beings to write and compile what we refer to as the Holy Bible, or God's Word. The Holy Spirit also guides and enables people like you and me to understand biblical truth.
7. The Bible, or what we sometimes call the Scriptures, points to and reveals Jesus Christ, gives an account of Jesus' life and ministry, and reveals God's will and purpose for humankind. The truth and authority of the Bible are without question; the Bible stands on its own.

The Bible, God's Word, clearly promises that each of us will indeed have a life hereafter, a life beyond this mortal life. Physical death will not be the end for us; we have something much more grand and glorious to look forward to.

A Life Hereafter?

"Then the King will say to those on his right, 'Come, you who are blessed by my Father; take your inheritance, the kingdom prepared for you since the creation of the world. For I was hungry and you gave me something to eat, I was thirsty and you gave me something to drink, I was a stranger and you invited me in, I needed clothes and you clothed me, I was sick and you looked after me, I was in prison and you came to visit me.' "Then the righteous will answer him, 'Lord, when did we see you hungry and feed you, or thirsty and give you something to drink? When did we see you a stranger and invite you in, or needing clothes and clothe you? When did we see you sick or in prison and go to visit you?' "The King will reply, 'I tell you the truth, whatever you did for one of the least of these brothers of mine, you did for me.'
—Matthew 25:34-40 NIV

"Then he will say to those on his left, 'Depart from me, you who are cursed, into the eternal fire prepared for the devil and his angels. For I was hungry and you gave me nothing to eat, I was thirsty and you gave me nothing to drink, I was a stranger and you did not invite me in, I needed clothes and you did not clothe me, I was sick and in prison and you did not look after me.' "They also will answer, 'Lord, when did we see you hungry or thirsty or a stranger or needing clothes or sick or in prison, and did not help you?' "He will reply, 'I tell you the truth, whatever you did not do for one of the least of these, you did not do for me.'
—Matthew 25:41-45 NIV

"Then they will go away to eternal punishment, but the righteous to eternal life."
—Matthew 25:46 NIV

In these passages, we see two distinct groups of people described. The righteous, or saved, are described in verses 34-40, and the cursed, or lost, are described in verses 41-45. Verse 46 then promises eternal life for the righteous (the saved, believers, saints, or Christians), but it promises everlasting punishment for the cursed (the lost, unsaved, wicked dead, or unbelievers). These promises are affirmed numerous times elsewhere in the Bible.

> For God so loved the world, that he gave his only begotten Son, that whosoever believeth in him should not perish, but have everlasting life.
> —John 3:16 KJV

The Bible refers to that place of eternal life as Heaven and to that place of everlasting punishment as Hell.

When the Bible speaks of life, or everlasting life, it generally is not referring to physical life, or mortal life. Instead, it usually is referring to spiritual life, a life that will become complete when a person attains Heaven. In a like manner, the Bible most often is alluding to spiritual death when it speaks of death, or perishing. That is the death a person experiences when he or she is relegated to Hell. More will be said about spiritual life and spiritual death in subsequent chapters of this book.

Chapter  3

HEAVEN

Is Heaven a real place? Will believers actually spend eternity there? The Bible clearly answers these questions with a resounding *yes*.

> Praise be to the God and Father of our Lord Jesus Christ! In his great mercy he has given us new birth into a living hope through the resurrection of Jesus Christ from the dead, and into an inheritance that can never perish, spoil or fade—kept in Heaven for you, who through faith are shielded by God's power until the coming of the salvation that is ready to be revealed in the last time.
> —1 Peter 1:3-5 NIV

> But when the time had fully come, God sent his Son, born of a woman, born under law, to redeem those under law, that we might receive the full rights of sons. Because you are sons, God sent the Spirit of his Son into our hearts, the Spirit who calls out, "Abba, Father." So you are no longer a

slave, but a son; and since you are a son, God has made you also an heir.

—Galatians 4:4-7 NIV

The "hope" we have in 1 Peter, chapter 1, verse 3, is not what we might refer to as wishful thinking or speculation. It is confident expectation based on the promises made to us in God's Word. The "last time" in verse 5 refers to the end of this age, judgment time, or when time as we know it ends and eternity begins. In His mercy and grace, God has given each believer spiritual life and has "birthed" each one into His family. As Christians, we thus become children of God, and as His children we are assured of an eternal home in Heaven in His glorious presence. That is our inheritance. Our hope, or confident expectation of eternity in Heaven, is accomplished through the resurrection of Jesus Christ from the dead. That fact will be discussed more fully in a later chapter of this book.

The human mind is unable to fully comprehend the true meaning of eternity in Heaven. We think in terms of things that are limited by time and space, but eternity in Heaven is not constrained by time and space. Our lack of understanding, however, does not make Heaven any less real.

In my Father's house are many mansions: if it were not so, I would have told you. I go to prepare a place for you.

—John 14:2 KJV

This "place" promised by our Lord Jesus Christ is what the Scriptures refer to as Heaven.

We have established the fact that God is preparing an eternal home for us, the place we call Heaven. That leads to our next big question, "What will Heaven be like?" Again, we turn to the Bible for our answer.

Heaven

> And I heard a great voice out of Heaven saying, Behold, the tabernacle of God is with men, and he will dwell with them, and they shall be his people, and God himself shall be with them, and be their God. And God shall wipe away all tears from their eyes; and there shall be no more death, neither sorrow, nor crying, neither shall there be any more pain: for the former things are passed away.
> —Revelation 21:3–4 KJV

In these verses and elsewhere in the Bible, we find Heaven described as being in the presence of God Himself. So, the very essence of Heaven is that believers will be in God's glorious presence forever and forever.

Do we really comprehend the glory of God's presence and just how awesome and wonderful Heaven will be? The apostle Paul answers that question for us.

> But as it is written, Eye hath not seen, nor ear heard, neither have entered into the heart of man, the things which God hath prepared for them that love him.
> —1 Corinthians 2:9 KJV

This verse seems to tell us that the human heart and intellect cannot imagine what Heaven will be like and that we have never heard or seen anything comparable to Heaven. But is that the way most Christians perceive Heaven? No, we tend to envision Heaven in terms of things that are precious and pleasing to us in this life. We visualize streets paved with gold, great buildings adorned with precious stones, and a place free of pain and sorrow. That perception is based on various passages of Scripture, primarily those found in the Book of Revelation.

> And I saw a new Heaven and a new earth: for the first Heaven and the first earth were passed away; and there was no more sea.... And he carried me away in the spirit to a great and

high mountain, and shewed me that great city, the holy Jerusalem, descending out of Heaven from God.... And the wall of the city had twelve foundations, and in them the names of the twelve apostles of the Lamb.... And the building of the wall of it was of jasper: and the city was pure gold, like unto clear glass. And the foundations of the wall of the city were garnished with all manner of precious stones.... And the twelve gates were twelve pearls; every several gate was of one pearl: and the street of the city was pure gold, as it were transparent glass.
—Revelation 21:1, 10, 14, 18–19a, 21 KJV

The revelation of Jesus Christ, which God gave unto him, to shew unto his servant things which must shortly come to pass: and he sent and signified it by his angel unto his servant John:....
—Revelation 1:1 KJV

The writer of the Book of Revelation described the New Jerusalem (Heaven) in terms of things that have great value and things of awesome splendor and beauty in this life. But is his description of Heaven a literal one or a symbolic one? That question is answered in the first verse of the Book of Revelation. John states in chapter 1, verse 1, that the "things which must shortly come to pass" were "signified" to him by the angel of the Lord. Therefore, the description of Heaven in the Book of Revelation is a symbolic one rather than a literal one. The apostle Paul affirms that conclusion in First Corinthians, chapter 2, verse 9, when he tells us that the human mind cannot comprehend what God has prepared for us in Heaven. So, I believe Heaven will be more glorious than the human mind can imagine. Words do not exist to adequately describe Heaven, and if they did, the mind of man could not comprehend them. The Holy Spirit-inspired authors of the Bible simply used the very best language at their disposal in describing the unspeakable beauty and glory of Heaven.

Heaven

Perhaps we can get a glimpse of Heaven by considering the Garden of Eden before Adam and Eve ate of the forbidden fruit and introduced sin into the human race.

> So God created man in his own image, in the image of God he created him; male and female he created them. God blessed them and said to them, "Be fruitful and increase in number; fill the earth and subdue it. Rule over the fish of the sea and the birds of the air and over every living creature that moves on the ground." Then God said, "I give you every seed-bearing plant on the face of the whole earth and every tree that has fruit with seed in it. They will be yours for food. And to all the beasts of the earth and all the birds of the air and all the creatures that move on the ground—everything that has the breath of life in it—I give every green plant for food." And it was so. God saw all that he had made, and it was very good. And there was evening, and there was morning—the sixth day.
> —Genesis 1:27-31 NIV

> The Lord God took the man and put him in the Garden of Eden to work it and take care of it.
> —Genesis 2:15 NIV

After creating humankind, God looked at all of His creation and said it was "very good"; indeed it was perfect. God then blessed humankind and gave them dominion over His perfect creation. Man was to work, but it was not toilsome labor. It was a joyful and pleasant labor of love for the Lord, taking care of His creation. The first two human beings lived in a paradise where conditions were ideal. They enjoyed God's daily presence and fellowship, they were happy in a God-ordained husband and wife relationship, all their needs were provided for, they lived in a lush garden of unspeakable beauty, their work was fruitful and pleasant, and they must have believed it would last forever.

Looking Toward Eternity: A Life Hereafter?

Surely, Heaven must be somewhat like this seemingly perfect setting in the original Garden of Eden. There was, however, at least one imperfection in the Garden of Eden at the time of humankind's first sin. Evil existed in the garden in the person of the serpent, or Satan.

> Now the serpent was more subtil than any beast of the field which the Lord God had made. And he said unto the woman, Yea, hath God said, ye shall not eat of every tree of the garden?
> —Genesis 3:1 KJV

In Heaven, believers will be free from the presence of evil, so Heaven will be an even better place than the Garden of Eden.

Note in Genesis, chapter 2, verse 15, that God made Adam caretaker of the Garden of Eden. He was to work in the garden, but it would not be unpleasant and toilsome labor. Instead, it would be joyful and satisfying work. Perhaps this is an indication of what believers will be doing in Heaven. This suggests that our eternity in Heaven may well be devoted to pleasant and fulfilling labor for the Lord. Come to think of it, what is more satisfying and fulfilling in our mortal lives than laboring for the Lord? My experience has been that some of my greatest blessings from God come when I am obedient to His will for my life and faithful in doing the "work" He has called me to do.

Chapter  4

HELL

We have determined that Heaven is a real place and that believers will spend eternity there in the glorious presence of God. It follows that if there is an everlasting home for the saved, there must also be an eternal home for unbelievers. The Bible affirms that truth.

> God is just: He will pay back trouble to those who trouble you and give relief to you who are troubled, and to us as well. This will happen when the Lord Jesus is revealed from Heaven in blazing fire with his powerful angels. He will punish those who do not know God and do not obey the gospel of our Lord Jesus. They will be punished with everlasting destruction and shut out from the presence of the Lord and from the majesty of his power on the day he comes to be glorified in his holy people and to be marveled at among all those who have believed.
> —2 Thessalonians 1:6–10a NIV

> Do not be afraid of those who kill the body but cannot kill the soul. Rather, be afraid of the One who can destroy both soul and body in Hell.
> —Matthew 10:28 NIV

The place of this everlasting destruction, or punishment, is what the Scriptures refer to as Hell. The very essence of Hell is that unbelievers will be separated from God and His glory forever, and that they will be in the presence of Satan, or the devil, for evermore.

> "Then he will say to those on his left, 'Depart from me, you who are cursed, into the eternal fire prepared for the devil and his angels.'.... Then they will go away to eternal punishment, but the righteous to eternal life."
> —Matthew 25:41, 46 NIV

Hell is defined by our Lord Jesus Himself in these verses as a place of eternal fire, or punishment, in the presence of the devil.

We have concluded that the human mind cannot comprehend the awesome beauty and glory of Heaven. Although the Scriptures are not as explicit regarding punishment in Hell, I also believe that mortal man is unable to fathom the terrible torment and suffering that will befall the unsaved in Hell. Once again, the authors of the Bible used the very best language available to them in describing Hell and its everlasting punishment of the lost.

> And I saw the dead, great and small, standing before the throne, and the books were opened. Another book was opened, which is the book of life. The dead were judged according to what they had done as recorded in the books. The sea gave up the dead that were in it, and death and Hades gave

up the dead that were in them, and each person was judged according to what he had done. Then death and Hades were thrown into the lake of fire. The lake of fire is the second death. If anyone's name was not found written in the book of life, he was thrown into the lake of fire.
—Revelation 20:12-15 NIV

"But the cowardly, the unbelieving, the vile, the murderers, the sexually immoral, those who practice magic arts, the idolaters and all liars–their place will be in the fiery lake of burning sulfur. This is the second death."
—Revelation 21:8 NIV

In these verses, Hell is referred to as the "lake of fire," the "fiery lake of burning sulfur," and the "second death." As used herein, second death means spiritual death, or eternal separation from God. Implicit in the various names used for Hell in the Bible are the horrible and unspeakable torment and punishment for unbelievers, including their separation from God forever. The "book of life" in these verses contains the names of all believers, and they are the only ones who will not spend eternity in Hell. Note that "the books" in Revelation, chapter 20, verse 12, contain the deeds, or works, of the unsaved. The significance of works of unbelievers will be discussed in subsequent chapters of this book.

Chapter  5

END-TIME JUDGMENTS

We find references to judgments throughout the Bible, for both believers and unbelievers. With regard to Heaven and Hell, these judgments are for the most part referred to as end-time judgments, or judgments at the end of this age. Most Bible scholars agree that this age will conclude with the Second Coming of Christ, with time as we know it coming to an end and with eternity beginning. We have questions pertaining to just what events will occur at the end of this age and what their sequence will be, and the answers depend on our particular interpretation of Scripture, primarily those related passages found in the Book of Revelation. The view shared by this writer, as reflected in the analysis herein, is that the end of time will be ushered in by the events outlined in the remainder of this chapter.

Keep in mind there is ample room for disagreement in interpreting the Book of Revelation. For example, many Bible students believe the Judgment Seat of Christ and the Great White Throne Judgment are two different judgments, separated by approximately one thousand years in time. Others maintain, however, that the Judgment Seat of Christ and the Great White Throne Judgment are in fact the same event. The validity of the analysis and conclusions presented in this book is not compromised if either view is adopted. What is important is that the purpose and nature of both judgments be considered in the analysis and conclusions. There may be other similar areas subject to disagreement and debate, but do not let such inconsequential differences in interpretation cloud your comprehension of the overall purpose and nature of the events surrounding the end-time judgments. In essence, let us agree to disagree as we endeavor to understand more clearly those key events that will occur at the end of this age.

But first let us address and clarify a major truth presented in the Bible, one that will help us define more clearly the purpose of the end-time judgments. Our ultimate destination of either Heaven or Hell will not be determined at the end-time judgments. Instead, that determination will be made before we depart this mortal life, before our physical deaths. Since the fall of man in the Garden of Eden, when Adam and Eve ate of the forbidden fruit and thus disobeyed God, all humanity has inherited the nature and an environment inclined to sin. Quite simply, it is our human nature to sin.

> For all have sinned and fall short of the glory of God....
> —Romans 3:23 NIV

> For the wages of sin is death, but the gift of God is eternal life in Christ Jesus our Lord.
> —Romans 6:23 NIV

All of us have sinned, and because God hates sin, our sin has separated us from Him. The penalty (wages) for our sin is spiritual death, eternal separation from God, and eternity in Hell.

End-Time Judgments

It would appear then that all of humanity is doomed to everlasting Hell. But God, in His love and mercy toward us, made provision to free us from the death penalty resulting from our sin.

> But God demonstrates his own love for us in this: While we were still sinners, Christ died for us.
> —Romans 5:8 NIV

> For God so loved the world, that he gave his only begotten Son, that whosoever believeth in him should not perish, but have everlasting life.
> —John 3:16 KJV

> That if you confess with your mouth, "Jesus is Lord," and believe in your heart that God raised him from the dead, you will be saved....For, "Everyone who calls on the name of the Lord will be saved."
> —Romans 10:9, 13 NIV

Through His sacrificial death on the cross at Calvary, Jesus paid our sin debt and thus provided a way for us to be reconciled to God. By believing in Jesus Christ, God's Son, we can have eternal life; we can be saved. It is of vital importance to note that in no way do we earn our salvation, that we cannot "work" our way into Heaven.

> For it is by grace you have been saved, through faith—and this not from yourselves, it is a gift of God—not by works, so that no one can boast. For we are God's workmanship, created in Christ Jesus to do good works, which God prepared in advance for us to do.
> —Ephesians 2:8–10 NIV

Looking Toward Eternity: A Life Hereafter?

We obtain our salvation by God's grace (His unmerited favor toward us), through our faith in Jesus Christ, so that we can do the work God has for us. God saves us to do good works.

Now, let us return to the end-time judgments. I believe as most Bible scholars do that the end of this age will be ushered in by the Second Coming of Christ.

> Brothers, we do not want you to be ignorant about those who fall asleep, or to grieve like the rest of men, who have no hope. We believe that Jesus died and rose again and so we believe that God will bring with Jesus those who have fallen asleep in him. According to the Lord's own word, we tell you that we who are still alive, who are left till the coming of the Lord, will certainly not precede those who have fallen asleep. For the Lord himself will come down from Heaven, with a loud command, with the voice of the archangel and with the trumpet call of God, and the dead in Christ will rise first. After that, we who are still alive and are left will be caught up together with them in the clouds to meet the Lord in the air. And so we will be with the Lord forever. Therefore encourage each other with these words.
> —1 Thessalonians 4:13–18 NIV

> Therefore judge nothing before the appointed time; wait till the Lord comes. He will bring to light what is hidden in darkness and will expose the motives of men's hearts. At that time each will receive his praise from God.
> —1 Corinthians 4:5 NIV

It seems that many first-century Christians, including the apostles, expected Christ to return during their lifetimes. Some were concerned about what would happen to the Christians that would die before Christ's return. In these passages, Paul did affirm the return of our Lord Jesus Christ, and he assured the believers at Thessalonica, and us, that those who had already

End-Time Judgments

died would not be left out. They would be raised to join our Lord in the air. Then, those believers still alive when Jesus returns will also be caught up together to meet Christ in the air. All saved people will thus be with the Lord forever. This event is what many refer to as the rapture of the Church, with "church" being defined as the universal church, which is composed of all believers throughout the history of mankind.

A logical question now is, "When will Christ return?" That question has been debated by Bible students for centuries, beginning at the time of Christ's ascension into the air subsequent to His resurrection. Jesus' disciples expected Him to establish an earthly kingdom, but they expected a military and political kingdom that would free the Israelites from Roman rule. And, they expected that kingdom to be established during their lifetimes. Prior to His ascension, Jesus told His disciples that only the Father knew when He would return to usher in the end of this age and establish His kingdom.

> So when they met together, they asked him, "Lord, are you at this time going to restore the kingdom to Israel?" He said to them: "It is not for you to know the times or dates the Father has set by his own authority. But you will receive power when the Holy Spirit comes on you; and you will be my witnesses in Jerusalem, and in all Judea and Samaria, and to the ends of the earth." After he said this, he was taken up before their very eyes, and a cloud hid him from their sight. They were looking intently up into the sky as he was going, when suddenly two men dressed in white stood beside them. "Men of Galilee," they said, "why do you stand here looking into the sky? This same Jesus, who has been taken from you into Heaven, will come back in the same way you have seen him go into Heaven."
>
> —Acts 1:6–11 NIV

Looking Toward Eternity: A Life Hereafter?

> "Heaven and earth will pass away, but my words will never pass away. No one knows about that day or hour, not even the angels in Heaven, nor the Son, but only the Father. As it was in the days of Noah, so it will be at the coming of the Son of Man. For in the days before the flood, people were eating and drinking, marrying and giving in marriage, up to the day Noah entered the ark; and they knew nothing about what would happen until the flood came and took them all away. That is how it will be at the coming of the Son of Man. Two men will be in the field; one will be taken and the other left. Two women will be grinding with a hand mill; one will be taken and the other left. "Therefore keep watch, because you do not know on what day your Lord will come. But understand this: If the owner of the house had known at what time of the night the thief was coming, he would have kept watch and would not have let his house be broken into. So you also must be ready, because the Son of Man will come at an hour when you do not expect him."
> —Matthew 24:35-44 NIV

In these verses, Jesus refers to Himself as the Son of Man as He predicts His return at the end of this age. Many would-be Bible scholars have predicted specific dates or time periods for Christ's second coming. Some have staked their predictions on complicated and detailed calculations based on their interpretations of somewhat vague Bible passages. Others have claimed personal revelations from God as the basis of their predictions of the dates for Christ's return. Down through the centuries, time has shown all the previously predicted dates of Christ's second coming to be false. I believe time will also prove any future predicted date of Christ's return to be false. I do not know about you, but I take Jesus at His word when He tells us in Acts, chapter 1, verse 7, and in Matthew, chapter 24, verse 36, that no person knows the date of His second coming. Jesus has not returned yet, but we do know that God's Word promises He will return at some time in the future. That is good enough for me.

So, how can we be ready for the Second Coming of Christ if we do not know when it will be or if it will be in our lifetime? We know His return is imminent; it can be at any time, and it will be at a time when we do not expect it. That tells us we should be ready at all times for His return, but what does being ready mean? I believe the answer to that question is found in Acts, chapter 1, verse 8, and in Matthew, chapter 24, verse 42. We must be faithful and busy doing the work God has called us to do. Each of us must stay busy ministering to people's needs in Jesus' name and witnessing for Him. We should start in our neighborhoods and reach out to the entire world. This includes both individual work and cooperative efforts by groups of believers.

The Bible tells us repeatedly that each of us, believers and unbelievers alike, will be held accountable to God for everything we have done, both good and bad. It is thus certain that all of us will face God's end-time judgment. Numerous Bible scholars believe both the saved and the lost will be judged at the same time in a general judgment. But others believe there will be separate judgments for believers and unbelievers. This writer shares the latter view, and that will be the view incorporated herein. We must remember, though, that the times of these judgments are of secondary importance. The purpose and nature of judgments for both the saved and the lost are of utmost importance.

The first judgment to be considered is what the New Testament refers to as the "Judgment Seat of Christ." I believe that it will be for the saved only and that it will take place shortly after all believers meet Christ in the air at His second coming.

Looking Toward Eternity: A Life Hereafter?

> For we must all appear before the judgment seat of Christ; that every one may receive the things done in his body, according to that he hath done, whether it be good or bad.
> —2 Corinthians 5:10 KJV

> But why dost thou judge thy brother? Or why dost thou set at nought thy brother? For we shall all stand before the judgment seat of Christ.
> —Romans 14:10 KJV

The Judgment Seat of Christ will not be a judgment of sin to determine if a person is to be sent to Heaven or to Hell. Instead, it will be a judgment of a Christian's works, or deeds, to determine that individual's rewards, or lack of rewards, in Heaven. More will be said in the following chapter about believers' rewards.

How do we know that the Judgment Seat of Christ will be for believers only? The first indication is that the apostle Paul's second letter to the Corinthians was addressed to the church at Corinth and to the saints, or believers, in all Achaia.

> Paul, an apostle of Christ Jesus by the will of God, and Timothy our brother, to the church of God in Corinth, together with all the saints throughout Achaia....
> —2 Corinthians 1:1 NIV

So, since the letter was addressed only to saints, the pronoun "we" in chapter 5, verse 10 must also apply only to believers. In addition, closer examination of chapter 5 of Second Corinthians reveals that the pronoun "we" is used in more than twenty other places, and in each case it refers only to believers.

The next major end-time event of interest is the "Thousand-Year Millennium," in which Jesus Christ Himself will reign with His saints.

End-Time Judgments

> And I saw an angel come down from Heaven, having the key of the bottomless pit and a great chain in his hand. And he laid hold on the dragon, that old serpent, which is the Devil, and Satan, and bound him a thousand years, And cast him into the bottomless pit, and shut him up, and set a seal upon him, that he should deceive the nations no more, til the thousand years should be fulfilled: and after that he must be loosed a little season.
> —Revelation 20:1-3 KJV

> Blessed and holy is he that hath part in the first resurrection: on such the second death hath no power, but they shall be priests of God and of Christ, and shall reign with him a thousand years. And when the thousand years are expired, Satan shall be loosed out of his prison,....
> —Revelation 20:6-7 KJV

There is widespread disagreement among Bible scholars regarding the exact nature of the Thousand-Year Millennium, or the Millennial Kingdom. It is beyond the scope of this book to attempt to prove that there will indeed be a literal thousand-year millennium or to define it in any detail. Let us make note, however, of two significant points in the above Scripture passage. The "first resurrection" in verse 6 refers to that time when believers will be raised to be with Christ at His second coming. A lot more will be said about the first resurrection in a later chapter of this book on the resurrection of the body. Also in verse 6, "second death" refers to the spiritual death to be experienced by the lost when they are relegated to Hell for everlasting punishment. Obviously, believers will not experience this second death.

At the conclusion of the Thousand-Year Millennium, the unsaved will appear before the "Great White Throne Judgment." This will not be a judgment to determine whether or not a person is going to Hell. That decision was made when that person rejected Jesus Christ as his or her personal Savior and Lord and thus doomed himself or herself to eternity in Hell.

Looking Toward Eternity: A Life Hereafter?

> Then I saw a great white throne and him who was seated on it. Earth and sky fled from his presence, and there was no place for them. And I saw the dead, great and small, standing before the throne, and books were opened. Another book was opened, which is the book of life. The dead were judged according to what they had done as recorded in the books.
> —Revelation 20:11-12 NIV

The purpose of the Great White Throne Judgment is to judge a lost person's deeds, or works, both good and bad, in order to determine that person's punishment in Hell. More will be said about the punishment of unbelievers in the next chapter of this book.

Eternity will begin after the Great White Throne Judgment, when every person will be relegated to either Heaven or Hell. Believers will be sent to Heaven only because they believed in Jesus Christ and accepted Him as their personal Savior and Lord. In a like manner, unbelievers will be doomed to eternity in Hell only because they rejected Jesus Christ and refused to accept Him as their personal Savior and Lord. An individual will not go to Heaven or Hell because of his or her works, or deeds, in the flesh.

Our study of end-time judgments has not included a lot of the details presented in the Book of Revelation. As pointed out earlier, the Book of Revelation utilizes symbolic language, and there is widespread disagreement as to the meaning of all the events, visions, and other things described in it. This writer's overall interpretation of the Book of Revelation and related Bible passages has yielded a particular sequence of major events, namely, the Second Coming of Christ, followed sequentially by the resurrection of believers, the Judgment Seat of Christ for the saved, the Thousand-Year Millennium, the Great White Throne Judgment for unbelievers, and relegation of all humankind to either eternity in Heaven or everlasting Hell. We have

End-Time Judgments

neglected numerous details related to and surrounding these major events.

The Book of Revelation is by far the most controversial book in the Bible, and it is extremely difficult to understand. But, its primary message is very simple. Jesus and His forces of good, or righteousness, will win the ultimate victory over the devil and his forces of evil. That outcome was assured when Christ won the victory over death and the grave through His resurrection from the dead after His death on the cross at Calvary. There are still battles to be fought, but the final outcome is assured. The conclusions from our study seem to be consistent with that primary message of the Book of Revelation.

We will touch briefly on a few of the other events and things included in the Book of Revelation, but we will not attempt to interpret their exact meaning. Many Bible students believe a seven-year period of tribulation will occur after the Second Coming of Christ and before the start of the Thousand-Year Millennium. That period is referred to as the "Great Tribulation."

> And he shall confirm the covenant with many for one week: and in the midst of the week he shall cause the sacrifice and the oblation to cease, and for the overspreading of abominations he shall make it desolate, even until the consummation, and that determined shall be poured upon the desolate.
> —Daniel 9:27 KJV

> And at that time shall Michael stand up, the great prince which standeth for the children of my people: and there shall be a time of trouble, such as never was since there was a nation even to that same time: and at that time thy people shall be delivered, every one that shall be found written in the book.
> —Daniel 12:1 KJV

Looking Toward Eternity: A Life Hereafter?

> And it shall come to pass, that in all the land, saith the Lord, two parts therein shall be cut off and die; but the third shall be left therein. And I will bring the third part through the fire, and will refine them as silver is refined, and will try them as gold is tried: they shall call on my name, and I will hear them: I will say, It is my people: and they shall say, The Lord is my God.
> —Zechariah 13:8–9 KJV

> For then shall be great tribulation, such as was not since the beginning of the world to this time, no, nor ever shall be. And except those days should be shortened, there should no flesh be saved: but for the elect's sake those days shall be shortened.
> —Matthew 24:21–22 KJV

This Great Tribulation will occur after the Church, which consists of all believers throughout the history of mankind, has been called up to meet Christ in the air at His second coming. Believers, therefore, will not experience the terrible suffering and destruction of the seven years of tribulation. From the Old Testament passages in the books of Daniel, Zechariah, and others, it appears that God's main purpose for the Great Tribulation is to bring judgment on the Jewish people. That judgment will be somewhat of a "refining process" for them, in which they will be "purified" so they can be God's chosen people again. Chapters 6–19 in the Book of Revelation comprise an exhaustive account of this tribulation period. All the seals, trumpets, visions, vials, and so forth described in those fourteen chapters symbolize the terrible judgments to be brought on the unsaved and on the Jewish people.

The seven-year tribulation period will be concluded with what is referred to as the "Battle of Armageddon." That will be a climactic battle between the forces of righteousness and the forces of evil.

End-Time Judgments

For they are the spirits of devils, working miracles, which go forth unto the kings of the earth and of the whole world, to gather them to the battle of that great day of God Almighty. ... And he gathered them together into a place called in the Hebrew tongue Armageddon.
—Revelation 16:14,16 KJV

And I saw Heaven opened, and behold a white horse; and he that sat upon him was called Faithful and True, and in righteousness he doth judge and make war. His eyes were as a flame of fire, and on his head were many crowns; and he had a name written, that no man knew, but he himself. And he was clothed with a vesture dipped in blood: and his name is called The Word of God. And the armies which were in Heaven followed him upon white horses, clothed in fine linen, white and clean. And out of his mouth goeth a sharp sword, that with it he should smite the nations: and he shall rule them with a rod of iron: and he treadeth the winepress of the fierceness and the wrath of Almighty God. And he hath on his vesture and on his thigh a name written, KING OF KINGS, AND LORD OF LORDS.
—Revelation 19:11-16 KJV

And I saw the beast, and the kings of the earth, and their armies, gathered together to make war against him that sat on the horse, and against his army. And the beast was taken, and with him the false prophet that wrought miracles before him, with which he deceived them that had received the mark of the beast, and them that worshiped his image. These both were cast alive into a lake of fire burning with brimstone. And the remnant were slain with the sword of him that sat upon the horse, which sword proceeded out of his mouth: and all the fowls were filled with their flesh.
—Revelation 19:19-21 KJV

In verses 14 and 16 of chapter 16, we see the forces of evil being gathered together at a place called Armageddon. Then, in chapter 19, verses 11–16, the writer, John, sees Christ and His army. The Battle of Armageddon is described in verses 19–21 of chapter 19. It will not really be a battle because the forces of evil will be utterly destroyed by Christ and His army.

After the Battle of Armageddon, Satan will be bound for a thousand years, and Christ's Millennial Kingdom will be established. Believers, those who will be resurrected at Christ's second coming, will reign with Him for a thousand years.

> And I saw an angel come down from Heaven, having the key of the bottomless pit and a great chain in his hand. And he laid hold on the dragon, that old Serpent, which is the Devil, and Satan, and bound him a thousand years, And cast him into the bottomless pit, and shut him up, and set a seal upon him, that he should deceive the nations no more, till the thousand years should be fulfilled: and after that he must be loosed a little season. And I saw thrones, and they sat upon them, and judgment was given unto them: and I saw the souls of them that were beheaded for the witness of Jesus, and for the Word of God, and which had not worshiped the beast, neither his image, neither had received his mark upon their foreheads, or in their hands; and they lived and reigned with Christ a thousand years. But the rest of the dead lived not again until the thousand years were finished. This is the first resurrection. Blessed and holy is he that hath part in the first resurrection: on such the second death hath no power, but they shall be priests of God and of Christ, and shall reign with him a thousand years.
> —Revelation 20:1–6 KJV

Many theologians question the validity of a literal thousand-year millennium. There are also many questions and considerable disagreement with regard to the nature of the Millennial Kingdom. For example, what role will the Jews have in that kingdom, and will evil be present in the kingdom with Satan bound for the

End-Time Judgments

thousand years? It is beyond the scope of this study to attempt to answer any of those questions or concerns.

At the end of the thousand years, Satan will be turned loose for a period of time. He will go out in the world and by deception gather an army to fight against Christ and His forces of good.

> And when the thousand years are expired, Satan shall be loosed out of his prison, And shall go out to deceive the nations which are in the four quarters of the earth, Gog and Magog, to gather them together to battle: the number of whom is as the sand of the sea. And they went up on the breadth of the earth, and compassed the camp of the saints about, and the beloved city: and fire came down from God out of Heaven, and devoured them. And the Devil that deceived them was cast into the lake of fire and brimstone, where the beast and the false prophet are, and shall be tormented day and night for ever and ever. And I saw a great white throne, and him that sat on it, from whose face the earth and the Heaven fled away; and there was found no place for them.
> —Revelation 20:7–11 KJV

The army of Satan will be destroyed again by God, and Satan himself will be cast into the "lake of fire and brimstone," which is a reference to Hell. There, Satan will experience everlasting punishment. This final battle by Satan and his forces of evil against Christ and His saints will precede the Great White Throne Judgment, in which all unsaved people will be judged.

We may disagree on many of the interpretations and conclusions expressed in this chapter regarding end-time judgments, but let us agree on six vital points.

1. Jesus Christ will return to earth, and His coming will usher in the end of this age. Time as we know it will end, and eternity will begin.

2. Our ultimate destination of either Heaven for believers or Hell for unbelievers will not be determined at the Second Coming of Christ. That determination will be made before our physical deaths. If a person accepts Jesus Christ as his or her personal Savior and Lord, that person will attain Heaven. On the other hand, anyone refusing to accept Jesus Christ as his or her personal Savior and Lord will be relegated to Hell.
3. The deeds, or works, of believers will be judged to determine their rewards, or lack of rewards, in Heaven. Their good deeds in the flesh, along with the bad, will be included in this judgment.
4. The deeds in the flesh of the unsaved will also be judged. Their bad works, as well as the good, will be judged to determine their punishment in Hell.
5. Jesus Christ and His saints, the forces of righteousness, will win the ultimate victory over Satan and his forces of evil. There will be battles after Christ returns, but the ultimate victory was assured when Jesus Christ died on the cross at Calvary and then rose from the dead on Resurrection Morning.
6. All of humankind will be relegated to either eternal Heaven or everlasting Hell. The saved, or believers, will go to Heaven, and the lost, or unbelievers, will be doomed to Hell. There is no other option.

Chapter 6

DEGREES OF HEAVEN AND HELL

Most Christians agree there are, or will be, eternal destinations called Heaven and Hell, as set forth in the Bible. However, there are considerable differences in their perceptions of these everlasting "homes." The way in which they answer two basic questions reveals the diverse views they hold regarding Heaven and Hell.

1. Will Heaven be the same for all believers?
2. Will all unbelievers experience the same punishment in Hell?

Because our understanding of Heaven and Hell is limited by the capacity of our human minds, these are very difficult questions to answer. Let us examine several Scripture passages to see if the Bible can shed some light on this matter.

Some Bible students refer to differences in Heaven and differences in Hell, if they exist, as various levels of Heaven or

Hell. Others think of these differences as varying degrees of rewards in Heaven and varying degrees of punishment in Hell. A somewhat similar view held by additional Bible scholars is that residents of Heaven will have varying capacities to enjoy the full majesty and glory of Heaven, depending on their deeds (or works) in the flesh. In a like manner, residents of Hell will have different capacities to tolerate the horrendous torments of Hell, also depending on their deeds in the flesh. In our analysis, we assume the latter view wherein believers will have varying capacities to enjoy Heaven, and unbelievers will have different capacities to tolerate Hell. Our study results and conclusions would not be altered, however, if we chose one of the other views. Our particular approach to the study of this controversial issue will enable us to understand more clearly the significance of rewards and crowns in Heaven and punishment in Hell. Remember, though, that our human minds are incapable of comprehending fully what Heaven and Hell will be like.

Let us first consider as a simplified analogy a chess match between two master players with only two spectators in attendance. Assume the first spectator to be an accomplished chess player with a genuine interest in the outcome of the contest. On the other hand, the second spectator is assumed to be a novice chess player at best with virtually no interest in the outcome of the match. It is clear that both spectators would be watching the same chess match, but their comprehension and enjoyment of the contest would be vastly different. It would be because of the differences in their individual training and experience in chess that the two spectators would have totally different comprehension and enjoyment levels as they viewed the contest. The background and experience of the chess match spectators are somewhat analogous to our deeds, or works, in the flesh with regard to our capacity to enjoy Heaven or tolerate Hell. In a sense, you could say that our works in the flesh prepare us to enjoy Heaven or tolerate Hell. We will consider that to be degrees of rewards in Heaven and degrees of punishment in Hell.

I certainly do not understand what Heaven and Hell will be like, but I share the opinion of those who believe in degrees of rewards in Heaven and degrees of punishment in Hell. We will turn to several pertinent Scripture passages as we endeavor to develop a better understanding of what Heaven and Hell will be like. Let us not forget, though, that we are trying to comprehend the incomprehensible by viewing Heaven and Hell in light of things we can fathom. We will be discussing "rewards" and "crowns" in Heaven and "punishment" in Hell without any real knowledge as to what these terms really mean. We know only three things for certain about rewards and crowns in Heaven. They will come from God, they will be good, and they will be very desirable for the residents of Heaven. That is all we need to know. We also need to know only three things about unbelievers' punishment in Hell. It will be allowed by God, it will be bad, and it will be extremely undesirable for the residents of Hell. We are thus trying to gain a clearer understanding of the significance of rewards and crowns in Heaven and punishment in Hell without having any real knowledge regarding the actual meaning and nature of rewards, crowns, and punishment. This lack of knowledge does not invalidate our study results and conclusions, however.

Let us first consider rewards for the saved in Heaven. Will Heaven be the same for a lifelong and dedicated believer such as the apostle John and a "deathbed Christian" like the penitent thief on the cross beside Jesus?

> And one of the malefactors which were hanged railed on him, saying, If thou be Christ, save thyself and us. But the other answering rebuked him, saying, Dost not thou fear God, seeing thou art in the same condemnation? And we indeed justly; for we receive the due reward of our deeds: but

this man hath done nothing amiss. And he said unto Jesus, Lord, remember me when thou comest into thy kingdom. And Jesus said unto him, Verily I say unto thee, To day shalt thou be with me in paradise.
> —Luke 23:39-43 KJV

If Heaven is going to be the same for the apostle John and the penitent thief, then the rewards and crowns promised in the Scriptures seem to have no significance.

We have discussed in a previous chapter of this book the Judgment Seat of Christ, wherein a believer's works will be judged to determine the rewards in Heaven that will be given to or withheld from that believer.

> For we must all appear before the judgment seat of Christ; that every one may receive the things done in his body, according to that he hath done, whether it be good or bad.
> —2 Corinthians 5:10 KJV

> If any man builds on this foundation using gold, silver, costly stones, wood, hay or straw, his works will be shown for what it is, because the Day will bring it to light. It will be revealed with fire, and the fire will test the quality of each man's work. If what he has built survives, he will receive his reward. If it is burned up, he will suffer loss; he himself will be saved, but only as one escaping through the flames.
> —1 Corinthians 3:12-15 NIV

> And, behold, I come quickly; and my reward is with me, to give every man according as his work shall be.
> —Revelation 22:12 KJV

> But without faith it is impossible to please him: for he that cometh to God must believe that he is, and that he is a rewarder of them that diligently seek him.
>
> —Hebrew 11:6 KJV

I perceive the Judgment Seat of Christ as somewhat of a "balancing of the books." A believer's good deeds will be weighed against the bad, and the result will determine what that believer will receive in the way of rewards in Heaven. Note in First Corinthians, chapter 3, verse 15, that a believer will not lose his salvation because of his works, but he will lose some of his rewards. His salvation was secured when he believed in Jesus Christ and accepted Him as his personal Savior and Lord. For purposes of this study, the receiving of rewards or the withholding of rewards in Heaven is considered simply as different degrees of Heaven.

As noted before, some Bible scholars insist that Heaven will be the same for all believers. That view poses some questions for me. If Heaven will be exactly the same for everyone, what is the significance of rewards and crowns? Our rewards will be based on our works in the flesh, and we will have differing works, so how can our rewards be the same? If Heaven will indeed be the same for all Christians, tell me then how some residents can be given rewards and crowns that will be different from those given to other residents. The same questions apply to those Bible students who believe Hell will be the same for all unbelievers. It is my opinion that perceiving Heaven and Hell in such a manner is not consistent with the many promises in the Bible pertaining to rewards and crowns in Heaven and punishment in Hell.

There are several specific rewards promised in the Bible to some of the saved in Heaven. These are referred to as "crowns," and they will be given to particular believers according to their special service for the Lord. The first is the "Crown of Glory."

Looking Toward Eternity: A Life Hereafter?

> To the elders among you, I appeal as a fellow elder, a witness of Christ's sufferings and one who also will share in the glory to be revealed: Be shepherds of God's flock that is under your care, serving as overseers—not because you must, but because you are willing, as God wants you to be; not greedy for money, but eager to serve; not lording it over those entrusted to you, but being examples to the flock. And when the Chief Shepherd appears, you will receive the crown of glory that will never fade away.
> —1 Peter 5:1-4 NIV

This crown is clearly for the overseers and leaders of Christians in particular areas. It is for pastors, bishops, elders, and other leaders who have the spiritual overseer responsibility of a local congregation and who have performed their duties well. The duties of such an overseer are to love, feed, and care for his flock. The exact nature of the Crown of Glory, as well as the other crowns, is not explained in the Scriptures, but suffice to say they all can be considered as rewards in Heaven.

Another special reward, or crown, is the "Crown of Life." It will be given to those believers who have suffered unusual persecution and tribulations because of their faithfulness and their service for the Lord. Some Bible scholars also refer to this crown as the Martyr's Crown.

> Consider it pure joy, my brothers, whenever you face trials of many kinds, because you know that the testing of your faith develops perseverance. Perseverance must finish its work so that you may be mature and complete, not lacking anything. …Blessed is the man who perseveres under trial, because when he has stood the test, he will receive the crown of life that God has promised to those who love him.
> —James 1:2-4, 12 NIV

> "Do not be afraid of what you are about to suffer. I tell you, the devil will put some of you in prison to test you, and you will suffer persecution for ten days. Be faithful, even to the point of death, and I will give you the crown of life."
> —Revelation 2:10 NIV

The main theme of these verses is that Christians will surely face difficulties and trials of various kinds as we live out our faith. And, that we should persevere in the midst of all our tribulations, placing our hope in Jesus Christ and trusting that He will be with us as we go through our trials and difficulties. The Crown of Life could also be interpreted to mean everlasting life, which will be given to all believers, but I believe the Crown of Life will be reserved for those Christians who have had to endure unusual persecution and trials. It will be a special reward for their faithful service.

The next special reward to be considered is the "Crown of Rejoicing," or "Crown of Glorifying." It will be a crown given to Christians who have led others to a saving faith in Jesus Christ. It could be considered a soul winner's crown.

> For what is our hope, or joy, or crown of rejoicing? Are not even ye in the presence of our Lord Jesus Christ at his coming? For ye are our glory and joy.
> —1 Thessalonians 2:19–20 KJV

In earlier verses of First Thessalonians, chapter 2, the writer, Paul, had assured the believers at Thessalonica how important they were to him. It was the result of Paul's ministry that they had become believers in the Lord Jesus Christ. In verse 20, Paul called them his glory and joy, and he told them in verse 19 that it was because they would be in Christ's presence at His second coming that he would receive the Crown of Rejoicing.

Looking Toward Eternity: A Life Hereafter?

The "Incorruptible Crown" will be a special reward for those who run the race of life in a worthy manner, maintaining self-control and self-discipline as they live out their faith.

> Know ye not that they which run in a race run all, but one receiveth the prize? So run, that ye may obtain. And every man that striveth for the mastery is temperate in all things. Now they do it to obtain a corruptible crown; but we an incorruptible. I therefore so run, not as uncertainly; so fight I, not as one that beateth the air: But I keep under my body, and bring it into subjection: lest that by any means, when I have preached to others, I myself should be a castaway.
> —1 Corinthians 9:24–27 KJV

Paul compared the Christian life to an athletic contest. An athlete will maintain a strict training routine and practice the self-discipline necessary to win a contest. However, the crown he wins is temporary; it is corruptible. The Christian must also practice self-control and self-discipline to keep on track doing our Lord's work. Keeping on track means not yielding to worldly temptations, selfish desires of the flesh, and other interests and distractions that would hinder us from living a fruitful Christian life. Thus, by practicing self-control and maintaining discipline in our walk with the Lord, we can win an Incorruptible Crown, one that will endure forever.

The last special reward to be considered is the "Crown of Righteousness," which is somewhat similar to the Incorruptible Crown.

> For I am already being poured out like a drink offering, and the time has come for my departure. I have fought the good fight, I have finished the race, I have kept the faith. Now there is in store for me the crown of righteousness, which the Lord, the righteous judge, will award to me on that day—and not only to me, but also to all who have longed for his appearing.
> —2 Timothy 4:6–8 NIV

Degrees of Heaven and Hell

The apostle Paul was in prison in Rome awaiting his pending execution when he wrote his second letter to Timothy. After giving instructions to Timothy, Paul looked back over his many years as a faithful apostle of the Lord Jesus Christ. He felt he had fought the good fight in his ministry and he had accomplished the goals he had been striving for. He was not ashamed of the work he had done for the Lord, and he was looking forward to the time Christ would return. Paul believed he would receive the Crown of Righteousness at Christ's second coming. This crown will also be given to all believers who are not ashamed of their work for the Lord and who are looking forward to His return.

If there will indeed be different degrees of rewards in Heaven, it follows that there must also be different degrees of punishment in Hell. I believe the Scriptures do affirm that truth. In the same manner that believers will come before the Judgment Seat of Christ to be rewarded for their good works, I believe the wicked dead will come before the Great White Throne Judgment to determine the degrees of their punishment in Hell. Their punishment will result from their deeds of the flesh (works), both good and bad. This means that a lifelong evil unbeliever who has committed horrible crimes against humanity (such as a Hitler of World War II) will experience much greater torment in Hell than an unsaved person who has lived a "good" life helping others.

Remember that an unsaved person will be relegated to Hell solely because he or she did not believe in the Lord Jesus Christ and accept Him as his or her personal Savior and Lord. No one will be sent to Hell because of his or her works.

> For the Son of Man shall come in the glory of his Father with his angels; and then he shall reward every man according to his work.
>
> —Matthew 16:27 KJV

# Looking Toward Eternity: A Life Hereafter?

> Since you know that you will receive an inheritance from the Lord as a reward. It is the Lord Christ you are serving. Anyone who does wrong will be repaid for his wrong, and there is no favoritism.
> —Colossians 3:24–25 NIV

> And I saw a great white throne, and him that sat on it, from whose face the earth and the Heaven fled away; and there was found no place for them. And I saw the dead, small and great, stand before God; and the books were opened: and another book was opened, which is the book of life: and the dead were judged out of those things which were written in the books, according to their works.
> —Revelation 20:11–12 KJV

> And whosoever was not found written in the book of life was cast into the lake of fire.
> —Revelation 20:15 KJV

The "book of life" in these verses contains the names of all saved people, whose eternal destination is Heaven rather than Hell. The "books" in Revelation, chapter 20, verse 12, contain the works, or deeds, of the unsaved. The works of the lost will thus determine the degrees of their punishment in Hell. This difference in punishment is considered to mean different degrees of Hell.

Chapter 7

BETWEEN PHYSICAL DEATH AND THE END OF THIS AGE

What will happen to our souls immediately following our physical deaths? Will we attain our final destinations of Heaven or Hell before the Second Coming of Christ and the end of this age? Will we receive resurrected bodies, and if so, when will our souls be united with our resurrected bodies? In essence, what will happen to each of us between the moment of mortal death and the point in time when Christ returns? The Bible does not furnish simple and easy-to-understand answers to these questions. The result is that Bible students develop differing views and perceptions concerning this issue, and a substantial number of dedicated Christians become somewhat confused about this particular segment of our life hereafter. Equally confusing is the fact that a number of the diverse views held by serious Bible students can be supported to some extent by Scripture.

We will do well to remember we are attempting to comprehend certain aspects of Heaven and Hell even though we know the precise nature of Heaven and Hell are well beyond what the human mind can grasp. We are dealing with a finite time period at the end of this age, but we are also looking forward to eternity, which is not constrained by time as we know it. We are thus trying to blend a finite-time segment of our life hereafter with the eternal portion of our life beyond this mortal life, so our vision is cloudy at best.

We will examine several Bible passages as we endeavor to answer a few of the key questions pertaining to that "time period" immediately following our physical deaths. Keep in mind, though, that time as we know it will cease at the end of this age, so the time period we are considering will conclude with the Second Coming of Christ. We will link these various Bible passages together, allowing Scripture to interpret Scripture, as we arrive at what I suggest to be logical and reasonable answers to some of our questions regarding this initial segment of our life hereafter.

A vast majority of Christians believe a person's soul will leave that person's body at the moment of physical death. It is evident the physical body itself will not go anywhere at the moment of physical death. A further word of caution is in order at this time. The mortal mind can understand only those things constrained by time and space, so we do not fully comprehend things spiritual and eternal. We cannot see the soul or measure it; neither can we confirm its existence by scientific means, so we have to accept its reality on faith. God's Word reveals to us the existence of our souls, and we must rely on His Word to show us what will happen to them after we die.

Both Old Testament writers and New Testament authors thought of earth as their temporary homes. They considered themselves as sojourners, or strangers, passing through this brief mortal life to an everlasting life.

Between Physical Death and the End of This Age

> For we are strangers before thee, and sojourners, as were all our fathers: Our days on the earth are as a shadow, and there is none abiding.
> —1 Chronicles 29:15 KJV

> And if ye call on the Father, who without respect to persons judgeth according to every man's work, pass the time of your sojourning here in fear…
> —1 Peter 1:17 KJV

> For to me, to live is Christ and to die is gain. If I am to go on living in the body, this will mean fruitful labor for me. Yet what shall I choose? I do not know! I am torn between the two: I desire to depart and be with Christ, which is better by far; but it is more necessary for you that I remain in the body.
> —Philippians 1:21–24 NIV

The apostle Paul was undoubtedly looking forward to being with Christ after his physical death. He longed for that eternal life that would be far better than his mortal life, but he realized his life in the flesh must be prolonged until he had finished the work Christ had called him to do. Paul fully understood it would be desirable for him to die a physical death and be with the Lord, but it would be better for the Philippian believers for him to remain in the flesh. They needed him, and Paul was willing to place their needs above his desire to be with Christ. Paul longed for his permanent heavenly home, but he rightly placed a higher priority on serving the Lord as he lived out his mortal life as a sojourner, or stranger, in his earthly home.

We would do well to adopt Paul's philosophy in our own lives. Quite often, people with terminal illnesses, spouses grieving for lost mates, those suffering intense pain, or others with seemingly unbearable problems are ready to give up and depart this mortal life. We too should remember that God leaves us here for a reason, and we should be willing to serve Him in whatever way we can. Our priority should be on completing the work God has called us to do, because we have an eternity ahead of us in which we will be with the Lord.

We discussed briefly in chapter six the penitent thief on the cross beside Jesus. He was what we sometimes refer to as a "deathbed Christian," one who becomes a believer just prior to his physical death.

> And he said unto Jesus, Lord, remember me when thou comest into thy kingdom. And Jesus said unto him, Verily I say unto thee, To day shalt thou be with me in paradise.
> —Luke 23:42-43 KJV

Did Jesus mean the penitent thief's body would be with Him in Paradise that day? Certainly not! The thief's body would either remain on the cross that day or be taken down and placed in a grave. So, Jesus must have been referring to the thief's soul. We can conclude from this passage that our soul will depart from our body on the day of our physical death, and I also suggest it will occur at the precise moment of our mortal death.

The obvious question that arises from the preceding Bible passage is "What is, or where is, Paradise?" The Bible seems to portray Paradise as either being Heaven or being associated with Heaven in some way.

> I must go on boasting. Although there is nothing to be gained, I will go on to visions and revelations from the Lord. I know a man in Christ who fourteen years ago was caught up to the third Heaven. Whether it was in the body or out of the body I do not know—God knows. And I know that this man—whether in the body or apart from the body I do not know, but God knows—was caught up to paradise. He heard inexpressible things, things that man is not permitted to tell.
> —2 Corinthians 12:1-4 NIV

Between Physical Death and the End of This Age

Paul tells us that he had been caught up in some kind of vision to the Third Heaven, or Paradise. He did not know if he had been caught up in physical form or if it had been an out-of-body experience, but he was certain he had seen Paradise. This is most surely a reference to the place we call Heaven, the place where all Christians will spend eternity after the end of this age.

The apostle John described in great detail what he had seen in his vision of Heaven, as recorded in the Book of Revelation and discussed in chapter three herein. Paul did not attempt to explain in such detail what he had seen or heard in his vision. He merely stated that, "he heard inexpressible things, things that man is not permitted to tell." The implication is that the mind of man could not comprehend nor express what he had witnessed in his vision of Paradise. That is consistent with what we have concluded thus far about the unspeakable glory and majesty of Heaven.

In His message to the angel of the church at Ephesus, in chapter 2 of the Book of Revelation, Christ Himself referred to the "tree of life" in the "paradise of God."

> "He who has an ear, let him hear what the Spirit says to the churches. To him who overcomes, I will give the right to eat from the tree of life, which is in the paradise of God."
> —Revelation 2:7 NIV

> Blessed are they that do his commandments, that they may have right to the tree of life, and may enter in through the gates into the city.
> —Revelation 22:14 KJV

> And out of the ground made the Lord God to grow every tree that is pleasant to the sight, and good for food; the tree of life also in the midst of the garden, and the tree of knowledge of good and evil.
> —Genesis 2:9 KJV

Looking Toward Eternity: A Life Hereafter?

The apostle John includes the tree of life in his portrayal of Heaven in the Book of Revelation, chapter 22. We can thus conclude that Jesus was referring to Heaven when He talked about the Paradise of God. The tree of life in Heaven, as included in the description of Heaven in the Book of Revelation, reminds us of the tree of life in the Garden of Eden, as described in Genesis, chapter 2. That gives validity to our comparison of Heaven to the Garden of Eden in chapter three of this book.

So what do all these Scripture passages tell us regarding Paradise? First, I believe they tell the saved that each of our souls will depart from our physical body at the moment of mortal death. Our souls will then go to a place the Bible refers to as Paradise, which seems to be either Heaven, a part of Heaven, or a place in some way associated with Heaven. We cannot imagine what Heaven will be like; neither can we begin to understand Paradise. But suffice to say that Paradise, the initial residence of our souls subsequent to our mortal deaths, will be a glorious place of joy and bliss. Let me suggest also that a believer's soul will remain in Paradise until the Second Coming of Christ, at which time his or her soul will be united with his or her resurrected body. Resurrection of the body will be discussed at great length in the next chapter of this book.

We have thus concluded that a Christian's soul will be in Paradise between the time of his or her physical death and the Second Coming of Christ. But what about a lost person's soul? The Bible is not as clear with respect to an unbeliever's soul, but I believe that a similar but opposite fate awaits the soul of an unsaved person. I therefore suggest that an unbeliever's soul will depart from his or her body at the moment of mortal death and that it will go to either Hell or a place associated with Hell. The Scriptures do not give a name for this initial residence of an unbeliever's soul subsequent to his or her physical death, but I believe it is a place analogous to Paradise for Christians. Needless to say, it will be a place of unthinkable anguish and torment.

Between Physical Death and the End of This Age

Our conclusion regarding what will happen to us between our physical deaths and the end of this age is not explicitly grounded in Scripture. However, I believe our conclusion is consistent with Bible passages dealing with our mortal deaths, the Second Coming of Christ, our bodily resurrection, and our ultimate relegation to either Heaven or Hell. This is just another piece of the biblical puzzle that gives us a view of our life hereafter.

Chapter 8

RESURRECTION OF THE BODY

The Bible speaks clearly and with certainty of a resurrection for both believers and unbelievers. There is, however, a great deal of disagreement among Christians as to what resurrection really means. Many believe, as this writer does, that we will receive resurrected bodies, but others maintain that resurrection from the dead applies only to the soul. The Bible presents resurrection for the saved as being dependent on, and connected to, the resurrection of our Lord Jesus Christ. A study of the Scriptures confirms the certainty of Jesus' resurrection, the reality of bodily resurrection for both the saved and the unsaved, and the times of their resurrections.

Let us consider first the resurrection of Jesus after He had been crucified, laid in a tomb, and left in the grave for three days. A Roman guard had been posted to ensure no one tampered with the grave.

Looking Toward Eternity: A Life Hereafter?

As evening approached, there came a rich man from Arimathea, named Joseph, who had himself become a disciple of Jesus. Going to Pilate, he asked for Jesus' body, and Pilate ordered that it be given to him. Joseph took the body, wrapped it in a clean linen cloth, and placed it in his own new tomb that he had cut out of the rock. He rolled a big stone in front of the entrance to the tomb and went away. Mary Magdalene and the other Mary were sitting there opposite the tomb. The next day, the one after Preparation Day, the chief priests and the Pharisees went to Pilate. "Sir," they said, "we remember that while he was still alive that deceiver said, 'After three days I will rise again.' So give the order for the tomb to be made secure until the third day. Otherwise, his disciples may come and steal the body and tell the people that he has been raised from the dead. This last deception will be worse than the first." "Take a guard," Pilate answered. "Go, make the tomb as secure as you know how." So they went and made the tomb secure by putting a seal on the stone and posting the guard.

—Matthew 27:57–66 NIV

On the first day of the week, very early in the morning, the women took the spices they had prepared and went to the tomb. They found the stone rolled away from the tomb, but when they entered, they did not find the body of the Lord Jesus. While they were wondering about this, suddenly two men in clothes that gleamed like lightning stood beside them. In their fright the women bowed down with their faces to the ground, but the men said to them, "Why do you look for the living among the dead? He is not here; he has risen! Remember how he told you, while he was still with you in Galilee: 'The Son of Man must be delivered into the hands of sinful men, be crucified and on the third day be raised again.'"

—Luke 24:1–7 NIV

Resurrection of the Body

Jesus had told His followers He would be crucified but that He would be raised from the dead on the third day. A group of women took spices to Jesus' tomb early in the morning on the third day after His burial. Their purpose was to properly anoint Jesus' body, because they had been given insufficient time on the day of His crucifixion and burial to adequately prepare His body for burial. The women found an empty grave that morning, and two angels told them Jesus had risen from the dead, that He was alive. Jesus was the risen Lord.

On that same day, Jesus' disciples assembled together in a locked room in Jerusalem discussing the tragic events of the previous days and the troubling things they had heard concerning His being raised from the dead.

> While they were still talking about this, Jesus himself stood among them and said to them, "Peace be with you." They were startled and frightened, thinking they saw a ghost. He said to them, "Why are you troubled, and why do doubts rise in your minds? Look at my hands and my feet. It is I myself! Touch me and see; a ghost does not have flesh and bones, as you see I have." When he had said this, he showed them his hands and feet. And while they still did not believe it because of joy and amazement, he asked them, "Do you have anything here to eat?" They gave him a piece of broiled fish, and he took it and ate it in their presence.
> —Luke 24:36-43 NIV

> On the evening of that first day of the week, when the disciples were together, with the doors locked for fear of the Jews, Jesus came and stood among them and said, "Peace be with you!" After he said this, he showed them his hands and side. The disciples were overjoyed when they saw the Lord.
> —John 20:19-20 NIV

Looking Toward Eternity: A Life Hereafter?

Jesus appeared suddenly to His disciples inside the locked room. They were frightened and amazed, not yet realizing that Jesus was indeed raised from the dead. Jesus showed them His nail-scarred hands and feet, and He asked them to touch Him to verify He was truly flesh and bones. Jesus then ate some broiled fish in their presence to further affirm He really had a resurrected body.

We do not know just how Jesus' resurrected body differs from our mortal bodies, but we can glean some information from a study of key Scripture passages, such as:

> And when she had thus said, she turned herself back, and saw Jesus standing, and knew not that it was Jesus. Jesus saith unto her, Woman, why weepest thou? Whom seekest thou? She, supposing him to be the gardener, saith unto him, Sir, if thou have borne him hence, tell me where thou hast laid him, and I will take him away. Jesus saith unto her, Mary. She turned herself, and saith unto him, Rabboni; which is to say, Master.
>
> —John 20:14-16 KJV

Mary Magdalene was outside the empty tomb early in the morning when Jesus appeared to her. She did not recognize Him at first, but then Jesus called her by name and she knew who it was. This and other similar Bible passages tell us that Jesus could make Himself recognizable or unrecognizable at will. In addition, Jesus could appear or disappear at will. He appeared suddenly to His disciples in a locked room, apparently without coming in by way of the door, and He seemed to appear out of nowhere to Mary Magdalene at the tomb.

The Bible also tells us Jesus' resurrected body is immortal and incorruptible. This fact was proclaimed by King David in the Old Testament and confirmed by the writer of the Book of Acts in the New Testament.

Resurrection of the Body

> For thou wilt not leave my soul in Hell; neither wilt thou suffer thine Holy One to see corruption.
> —Psalm 16:10 KJV

> For David speaketh concerning him, I foresaw the Lord always before my face, for he is on my right hand, that I should not be moved: Therefore did my heart rejoice, and my tongue was glad; moreover also my flesh shall rest in hope: Because thou wilt not leave my soul in Hell, neither wilt thou suffer thine Holy One to see corruption. . . . He seeing this before spake of the resurrection of Christ, that his soul was not left in Hell, neither his flesh did see corruption. This Jesus hath God raised up, whereof we all are witnesses.
> —Acts 2:25-27, 31-32 KJV

We will see later in this chapter that believers will be given immortal, incorruptible, resurrected bodies like that of our Lord Jesus. The clear implication in Scripture is that Jesus' resurrected body is immortal and incorruptible, that He has won victory over death and the grave. That truth is affirmed throughout the New Testament.

Our resurrected Lord appeared to several individuals, He appeared to His disciples as a group, and He appeared to over five hundred of His followers at one time.

> For what I received I passed on to you as of first importance: that Christ died for our sins according to the Scriptures, that he was buried, that he was raised on the third day according to the Scriptures, and that he appeared to Peter, and then to the twelve. After that, he appeared to more than five hundred of the brothers at the same time, most of whom are still living, though some have fallen asleep. Then he appeared to James, then to all the apostles, and last of all he appeared to me also, as to one abnormally born.
> —1 Corinthians 15:3-8 NIV

Looking Toward Eternity: A Life Hereafter?

Note that in this passage the risen Lord appeared to believers only, those who had placed their faith in Him. The Bible does not record Jesus appearing to the unsaved after His resurrection. Perhaps that reveals to us the fact that Jesus' personal ministry of seeking out the lost had ended, that He would rely on His followers to perform that ministry for Him in the future. Jesus emphasized to His disciples that He was indeed in the flesh after He had risen from the grave, that He had received a resurrected body. The New Testament writers left no doubt that Jesus had died a physical death, that He had risen from the grave on the third day, and that He had been given a resurrected body.

Jesus did much more than just rise from the dead Himself. He won the victory over death and the grave and thus made it possible for believers to be resurrected from the dead to a life eternal.

> But now is Christ risen from the dead, and become the firstfruits of them that slept. For since by man came death, by man came also the resurrection of the dead. For as in Adam all die, even so in Christ shall all be made alive. But every man in his own order: Christ the firstfruits; afterward they that are Christ's at his coming.
> —1 Corinthians 15:20–23 KJV

> Marvel not at this: for the hour is coming, in the which all that are in the graves shall hear his voice, And shall come forth; they that have done good, unto the resurrection of life; and they that have done evil, unto the resurrection of damnation.
> —John 5:28–29 KJV

> But this I confess unto thee, that after the way which they call heresy, so worship I the God of my fathers, believing all things which are written in the law and in the prophets: And have hope toward God,

which they themselves also allow, that there shall be a resurrection of the dead, both of the just and unjust.
—Acts 24:14-15 KJV

These passages of Scripture affirm that Christ, as the first fruits, rose from the dead and, in doing so, He won victory over death and the grave. Two other all-important spiritual truths are also affirmed and clarified in these passages. First, this victory by Christ over death extends to all believers. We are all "made alive" in Christ; that is, we all shall be resurrected from the dead to everlasting life in Heaven. The resurrection of all the saved, "they that are Christ's," will occur at His second coming. The second truth is that believers are not the only ones to be resurrected. The unjust, or unsaved, will also be resurrected from the grave, but their resurrection will not be to eternal life in God's glorious presence. Theirs will be a resurrection to eternity in Hell, which is spiritual death, separated from our God forever.

The reality of a believers' resurrection is established and grounded in Scripture, but what does that resurrection actually mean? Will we be given resurrected bodies, or will resurrection apply only to our souls? Once again, let us turn to the Bible for our answer.

> Behold, I show you a mystery; We shall not all sleep, but we shall all be changed, In a moment, in the twinkling of an eye, at the last trump: for the trumpet shall sound, and the dead shall be raised incorruptible, and we shall be changed. For this corruptible must put on incorruption, and this mortal must put on immortality. So when this corruptible shall have put on incorruption, and this mortal shall have put on immortality, then shall be brought to pass the saying that is written, Death is swallowed up in victory.
> —1 Corinthians 15:51-54 KJV

Looking Toward Eternity: A Life Hereafter?

> That I may know him, and the power of his resurrection, and the fellowship of his sufferings, being made conformable unto his death; If by any means I might attain unto the resurrection of the dead.
> —Philippians 3:10-11 KJV

> But our citizenship is in Heaven. And we eagerly await a Savior from there, the Lord Jesus Christ, who, by the power that enables him to bring everything under his control, will transform our lowly bodies so that they will be like his glorious body.
> —Philippians 3:20-21 NIV

We have already concluded that Jesus was raised from the grave, that He was given an immortal, incorruptible, resurrected body. I believe these Scripture passages promise us that Christians will also receive immortal, incorruptible, resurrected bodies. Furthermore, our resurrected bodies will be "like unto His glorious body." Our bodies will be like that of our Lord Jesus Christ. We surely do not comprehend all that this immortal, incorruptible, resurrected body will encompass, but we know it will be perfect in every way.

The next question to be addressed is "When will this believer's resurrection take place?" Will it be at the moment of physical death, or will it occur at some later time? The Scriptures shed some light on this question as well.

> We believe that Jesus died and rose again and so we believe that God will bring with Jesus those who have fallen asleep in him. According to the Lord's own word, we tell you that we who are still alive, who are left till the coming of the Lord, will certainly not precede those who have fallen asleep. For the Lord himself will come down from Heaven, with a loud command, with the voice of the archangel and with the trumpet call of God, and the dead in Christ will rise first. After that,

Resurrection of the Body

> we who are still alive and are left will be caught up together with them in the clouds to meet the Lord in the air. And so we will be with the Lord forever.
> —1 Thessalonians 4:14-17 NIV

We determined in an earlier chapter that the souls of dead believers reside with Jesus in a place the Bible calls Paradise. So, I believe that "those who have fallen asleep in him" in verse 14 refers to those dead believers' souls in Paradise. The "coming of the Lord" in verse 15 will usher in the end of this age, and at that time our souls will be united with our resurrected bodies in the air. This means that each of us will receive our resurrected body at the Second Coming of Christ, which will be at some unknown time after our physical death.

We have found that the unsaved will also receive resurrected bodies, but their fate is vastly different from that of the saved. They will experience the "second death," which is eternity in Hell and separation from God forever.

> And I saw a great white throne, and him that sat on it, from whose face the earth and the Heaven fled away; and there was found no place for them. And I saw the dead, small and great, stand before God; and the books were opened: and another book was opened, which is the book of life: and the dead were judged out of those things which were written in the books, according to their works. And the sea gave up the dead which were in it; and death and Hell delivered up the dead which were in them: and they were judged every man according to their works. And death and Hell were cast into the lake of fire. This is the second death. And whosoever was not found written in the book of life was cast into the lake of fire.
> —Revelation 20:11-15 KJV

The Bible seems to be unclear with respect to the time when a lost person's soul will be united with his or her resurrected body.

Looking Toward Eternity: A Life Hereafter?

But I believe we know with certainty that it will be between the Second Coming of Christ and the time of the Great White Throne Judgment. The unsaved, those whose names are not found written in the book of life, will be cast into the lake of fire. This will be the second death, which means, quite simply, separation from God forever and eternity in Hell.

Chapter 9

CHRIST, BETWEEN THE CROSS AND THE RESURRECTION

We have determined that Jesus Christ was crucified, that He was placed in a grave, and that He was resurrected on the third day. This raises an interesting question that has puzzled Bible students for centuries. What happened to Jesus between the time He died on the cross at Calvary and the time He arose from the grave on Resurrection Morning? The Bible does not provide us with a clear and concise answer to that question. As a result, Bible students hold diverse views regarding that three-day gap between Jesus' mortal life and His life after resurrection. We will examine a number of Scripture passages as we attempt to gain a better understanding of what Jesus did in those three days.

Let us first review the primary mission of Jesus as the Incarnate Son of God and look at key events leading to and including His crucifixion. Doing so, I believe, will give us some insight with regard to Jesus' activity between the cross and His resurrection.

Looking Toward Eternity: A Life Hereafter?

The Word became flesh and made his dwelling among us. We have seen his glory, the glory of the One and Only, who came from the Father, full of grace and truth.

—John 1:14 NIV

"For I have come down from Heaven not to do my will but to do the will of him who sent me."

—John 6:38 NIV

"For the Son of Man came to seek and to save what was lost."

—Luke 19:10 NIV

"I give them eternal life, and they shall never perish; no one can snatch them out of my hand."

—John 10:28 NIV

In the past God spoke to our forefathers through the prophets at many times and in various ways, but in these last days he has spoken to us by his Son, whom he appointed heir of all things, and through whom he made the universe. The Son is the radiance of God's glory and the exact representation of his being, sustaining all things by his powerful word. After he had provided purification for sins, he sat down at the right hand of the Majesty in Heaven.

—Hebrews 1:1–3 NIV

"Do not think that I have come to abolish the Law or the Prophets; I have not come to abolish them but to fulfill them."

—Matthew 5:17 NIV

These Scripture passages tell us how God revealed Himself to humanity through the Word, His Incarnate Son, Jesus Christ. Jesus revealed God's character, His glory, and His power as He walked among mankind after His birth to the Virgin Mary.

Christ, Between the Cross and the Resurrection

Jesus the Son lived a sinless life, always obedient to the will of God the Father. His primary mission on earth was to provide a way of salvation to a sinful world. Jesus' sacrifice of Himself on the cross at Calvary made it possible for reconciliation between sinful humankind and God. Each of us was at one time separated from God because of our sins, and Jesus shed His blood as atonement for those sins. Jesus and His death on the cross are the way God chose to resolve the sin problem in our world, and He did so because of His love for us.

Jesus understood clearly His mission, and His ministry and His teaching always pointed to the cross. However, that does not mean Jesus desired to travel the cruel way of the cross. His prayer in the Garden of Gethsemane prior to His crucifixion tells us Jesus preferred some other way.

> Then Jesus went with his disciples to a place called Gethsemane, and he said to them, "Sit here while I go over there and pray." He took Peter and the two sons of Zebedee along with him, and he began to be sorrowful and troubled. Then he said to them, "My soul is overwhelmed with sorrow to the point of death. Stay here and keep watch with me." Going a little farther, he fell with his face to the ground and prayed, "My Father, if it is possible, may this cup be taken from me. Yet not as I will, but as you will."
> —Matthew 26:36-39 NIV

> Jesus went out as usual to the Mount of Olives, and his disciples followed him. On reaching the place, he said to them, "Pray that you will not fall into temptation." He withdrew about a stone's throw beyond them, knelt down and prayed, "Father, if you are willing, take this cup from me; yet not my will, but yours be done." An angel from Heaven appeared to him and strengthened him. And being in anguish, he prayed more earnestly, and his sweat was like drops of blood falling to the ground.
> —Luke 22:39-44 NIV

Looking Toward Eternity: A Life Hereafter?

Jesus was God in the flesh, but He was also fully human, so He experienced the same feelings and emotions that all humankind share. Jesus did not want to face death on the cross with all of its ramifications, so He prayed for the Father to remove that cup from Him. But, the Son was willing to accept the Father's will if crucifixion was the only way.

Death by crucifixion was the most cruel and inhumane means of execution in Jesus' day. It was so terrible the Roman authorities did not use it at all on their own citizens. Jesus' suffering and punishment included more than the terrible physical pain and agony He endured on the cross. Old Testament prophecy gives us some indication of the physical and mental abuse Jesus had to withstand.

> I offered my back to those who beat me, my cheeks to those who pulled out my beard; I did not hide my face from mocking and spitting.
> —Isaiah 50:6 NIV

> He was despised and rejected by men, a man of sorrows, and familiar with suffering. Like one from whom men hide their faces he was despised, and we esteemed him not....But he was pierced for our transgressions, he was crushed for our iniquities; the punishment that brought us peace was upon him, and by his wounds we are healed....He was oppressed and afflicted, yet he did not open his mouth; he was led like a lamb to the slaughter, and as a sheep before her shearers is silent, so he did not open his mouth....He was assigned a grave with the wicked, and with the rich in his death, though he had done no violence, nor was any deceit in his mouth....Therefore I will give him a portion among the great, and he will divide the spoils with the strong, because he poured out his life unto death, and was numbered with the transgressors. For he bore the sin of many, and made intercession for the transgressors.
> —Isaiah 53:3, 5, 7, 9, 12 NIV

Christ, Between the Cross and the Resurrection

These Suffering Servant passages from the Book of Isaiah foretell the rejection, ridicule, mockery, and physical abuse Jesus was to endure before He was actually crucified. This prophecy from Isaiah also points to the Suffering Servant, or Messiah, giving His life as an atonement for the sins of many. He bore the punishment for our sins when He was nailed to a cross at Calvary, and because of His sacrifice we can have peace with God.

Numerous New Testament passages describe the mental and physical anguish Jesus experienced before and during His crucifixion. Much of His persecution and suffering was fulfillment of prophecy in the Old Testament books of Isaiah and Psalms. Jesus had warned His disciples about the persecution and crucifixion that awaited Him in Jerusalem, but He also promised them He would be raised from the dead.

> Now as Jesus was going up to Jerusalem, he took the twelve disciples aside and said to them, "We are going up to Jerusalem, and the Son of Man will be betrayed to the chief priests and the teachers of law. They will condemn him to death and will turn him over to the Gentiles to be mocked and flogged and crucified. On the third day he will be raised to life!"
> —Matthew 20:17-19 NIV

> Then the high priest tore his clothes and said, "He has spoken blasphemy! Why do we need any more witnesses? Look, now you have heard the blasphemy. What do you think?" "He is worthy of death," they answered. Then they spit in his face and struck him with their fists. Others slapped him and said, "Prophesy to us, Christ. Who hit you?"
> —Matthew 26:65-68 NIV

> They stripped him and put a scarlet robe on him, and then twisted together a crown of thorns and set it on his head. They put a staff in his right hand and knelt in front of him and mocked him. "Hail, king of the Jews!" they said. They

spit on him, and took the staff and struck him on the head again and again. After they had mocked him, they took off the robe and put his own clothes on him. Then they led him away to crucify him.

—Matthew 27:28–31 NIV

The men who were guarding Jesus began mocking and beating him. They blindfolded him and demanded, "Prophesy! Who hit you?" and they said many other insulting things to him.

—Luke 22:63–65 NIV

Then Pilate took Jesus and had him flogged. The soldiers twisted together a crown of thorns and put it on his head. They clothed him in a purple robe and went up to him again and again, saying, "Hail, king of the Jews!" And they struck him in the face.

—John 19:1–3 NIV

Two robbers were crucified with him, one on his right and one on his left. Those who passed by hurled insults at him, shaking their heads and saying, "You who are going to destroy the temple and build it in three days, save yourself! Come down from the cross, if you are the Son of God!" In the same way the chief priests, the teachers of the law and the elders mocked him. "He saved others," they said, "but he can't save himself! He's the King of Israel! Let him come down now from the cross, and we will believe in him. He trusts in God. Let God rescue him now if he wants him, for he said, 'I am the Son of God.'" In the same way the robbers who were crucified with him also heaped insults on him.

—Matthew 27:38–44 NIV

The Jewish religious leaders had been plotting for some time to have Jesus killed. Judas Iscariot, one of Jesus' twelve disciples, agreed to betray Jesus for thirty pieces of silver. The chief priests and elders then sent an armed crowd to arrest Jesus. He was brought before the Jewish religious leaders first, and they sentenced Him to death. However, they had no authority to carry out such a death sentence, so they turned Jesus over to the Roman authorities. Initially, the Roman Governor of that province, Pontius Pilate, refused to have Jesus crucified. Finally, after a great amount of coercion by the Jews, Pilate agreed to crucify Jesus. He then turned Him over to Roman soldiers who carried out the sentence. The preceding Scripture passages describe in gruesome detail the mental and physical abuses Jesus had to endure from the Jewish religious leaders, the Roman soldiers, and those spectators watching His crucifixion. They mocked Him, beat Him with their fists, placed a crown of thorns on His head, spit on Him, clubbed Him with a staff, flogged Him, and hurled all kinds of insults at Him. The flogging in particular was so severe a punishment that many victims did not survive it.

Jesus had to endure cruel and inhumane treatment as He was tried, abused, and then crucified, and He had to face that terrible ordeal alone. All His disciples deserted Him out of fear for their own lives.

> Then Jesus told them, "This very night you will all fall away on account of me, for it is written: 'I will strike the shepherd, and the sheep of the flock will be scattered.' But after I have risen, I will go ahead of you into Galilee." Peter replied, "Even if all fall away on account of you, I never will." "I tell you the truth," Jesus answered, "this very night, before the rooster crows, you will disown me three times." But Peter declared, "Even if I have to die with you, I will never disown you." And all the other disciples said the same.
> —Matthew 26:31-35 NIV

> At that time Jesus said to the crowd, "Am I leading a rebellion, that you have come out with swords and clubs to capture me? Every day I sat in the temple courts teaching, and you did not arrest me. But this has all taken place that the writings

of the prophets might be fulfilled." Then all the disciples deserted him and fled.
—Matthew 26:55-56 NIV

Now Peter was sitting out in the courtyard, and a servant girl came to him. "You also were with Jesus of Galilee," she said. But he denied it before them all. "I don't know what you're talking about," he said. Then he went out to the gateway, where another girl saw him and said to the people there, "This fellow was with Jesus of Nazareth." He denied it again, with an oath: "I don't know the man!" After a little while, those standing there went up to Peter and said, "Surely you are one of them, for your accent gives you away." Then he began to call down curses on himself and he swore to them, "I don't know the man!" Immediately a rooster crowed. Then Peter remembered the word Jesus had spoken: "Before the rooster crows, you will disown me three times." And he went outside and wept bitterly.
—Matthew 26:69-75 NIV

During Jesus' last supper with His disciples, He stated that all of them would desert Him. Bold, outspoken Peter then boasted he would die before he deserted Jesus. Jesus, in turn, declared to Peter he would disown Him three times before the rooster crowed. Later that night, the armed crowd captured Jesus and all His disciples fled, just as Jesus had predicted. Peter was sitting in the courtyard at a distance during Jesus' trial before the Jewish religious leaders. Some of the people in the courtyard with Peter recognized him as one of Jesus' followers, but Peter emphatically denied it three times. Then the rooster crowed, and Peter remembered what Jesus had told him. The Bible tells us Jesus had to endure alone His trials before the Jewish religious leaders and the Roman authorities, the physical and mental abuse at their hands, and His crucifixion by Roman soldiers. His disciples had fled in fright at the time He needed them most.

Christ, Between the Cross and the Resurrection

We have seen how Jesus prayed in the Garden of Gethsemane for the Father to take the cup from Him. Was Jesus referring to the mental and physical abuses He expected to receive, the desertion by His disciples He knew was coming, or the agonizing physical death He faced on the cross? I believe the cup included all those things, but I believe the cup also included something of much greater significance.

> My God, my God, why have you forsaken me? Why are you so far from saving me, so far from the words of my groaning?
> —Psalm 22:1 NIV

> From the sixth hour until the ninth hour darkness came over all the land. About the ninth hour Jesus cried out in a loud voice, "*Eloi, Eloi, lama sabach-thani?*"—which means, "My God, my God, why have you forsaken me?"
> —Matthew 27:45-46 NIV

> When he had received the drink, Jesus said, "It is finished." With that, he bowed his head and gave up his spirit.
> —John 19:30 NIV

Shortly before His last breath, Jesus repeated the words of Psalm 22, "My God, my God, why have you forsaken me?" Then, He declared, "It is finished." I believe Jesus meant He was separated from the Father and that His redemptive mission on earth was successfully completed. I believe the most significant part of the cup Jesus asked the Father to remove was His spiritual separation from God the Father. That is what the Bible refers to as death (not mortal death, but spiritual death).

What did separation from God actually mean for Jesus? To answer that, let us consider why Jesus sacrificed Himself on the cross and what He accomplished in doing so. We will then be better able to answer the question.

Looking Toward Eternity: A Life Hereafter?

> For all have sinned and fall short of the glory of God....
> —Romans 3:23 NIV

> For the wages of sin is death, but the gift of God is eternal life in Christ Jesus our Lord.
> —Romans 6:23 NIV

These verses tell us all human beings have sinned, falling short of the standard God has set for us. The Bible also tells us the penalty for our sin is death, eternal separation from God. In a previous chapter about Heaven, we concluded that the very essence of Heaven is being in the glorious presence of God forever. Likewise, we concluded that the very essence of Hell is being separated from God eternally. So, our sins have earned us a place in Hell, separated from God forever. Fortunately, there is a way out for us.

> But God demonstrates his own love for us in this: While we were still sinners, Christ died for us.
> —Romans 5:8 NIV

> He himself bore our sins in his body on the tree, so that we might die to sins and live for righteousness; by his wounds you have been healed.
> —1 Peter 2:24 NIV

> For Christ died for sins once for all, the righteous for the unrighteous, to bring you to God. He was put to death in the body but made alive by the Spirit....
> —1 Peter 3:18 NIV

Jesus bore our sins on the cross at Calvary. He died as our substitute, an atonement for our sins; He purchased tickets into Heaven for us. Just what do the wages, or penalty, of our sin

Christ, Between the Cross and the Resurrection

consist of; what punishment do we earn? That punishment does not necessarily include the terrible physical and mental abuse Jesus endured prior to His crucifixion. Nor does it necessarily include desertion and rejection by all our friends. Neither does it include the agonizing death on the cross experienced by Jesus. The wages of our sin do include, however, separation from God, everlasting torment, and punishment in Hell. That tells us Jesus had to endure the eternal punishment of Hell to atone for our sins, to wipe the slate clean for us.

Now we address the big question, "What happened to Jesus between the time of His physical death on the cross and the time of His resurrection three days later?" To pay the penalty for our sins, Jesus had to spend eternity in Hell, but how could He do it in three days? None of us understands how that could be, but we must remember that Hell belongs to the spiritual realm. We are attempting to compare something temporal, a three-day time period, to eternal and spiritual things, in which time has no meaning. The Bible tells us we can't imagine the glory and bliss of Heaven or the torment and agony of Hell. We can comprehend only those things constrained by time and space, but in the spiritual realm time and space have no meaning. I can't explain how He accomplished it, but I truly believe Jesus somehow suffered the everlasting punishment of Hell because of my sins and your sins.

Some Bible students try to explain Jesus' activity between His death on the cross and His resurrection by their interpretation of key Scripture passages. Two passages in particular deal with Jesus' preaching to the spirits in prison.

> For Christ died for sins once for all, the righteous for the unrighteous, to bring you to God. He was put to death in the body but made alive by the Spirit, through whom also he went and preached to the spirits in prison....
> —1 Peter 3:18-19 NIV

Looking Toward Eternity: A Life Hereafter?

> For this is the reason the gospel was preached even to those who are now dead, so that they might be judged according to men in regard to the body, but live according to God in regard to the spirit.
> —1 Peter 4:6 NIV

We will not attempt to interpret these and other related Scripture passages. We will simply conclude that somehow Jesus managed to endure the everlasting punishment of Hell as our substitute, thus freeing us from the penalty of our sins.

Chapter 10

THE BIG PICTURE

All of us have to confront our mortality; each of us must face physical death. Most of us have probably wondered at one time or another if physical death is the end for us or if there is something beyond our mortal life. For thousands of years, the world's religions have addressed this most basic question of a life hereafter, and many diverse views have been developed regarding a life beyond this life. We have not attempted to examine the views of the various religions concerning a life hereafter. We have focused our study exclusively on the Judeo-Christian perspective of a life beyond this mortal life. We have turned to the Bible, God's Word, to establish the reality and nature of a life hereafter. In doing so, we have accepted on faith the truth and authority of the Bible. We are not required to prove that there is a God, that the Bible is His Word, that Jesus Christ is God's Incarnate Son, and that the Bible, or Scriptures, is complete truth. We must assume these four things to be true, and we must accept each one of them on faith.

Looking Toward Eternity: A Life Hereafter?

We have studied a number of Scripture passages dealing with a life hereafter, and we have considered key aspects of a life beyond this mortal life. Let us review briefly some of our previous conclusions and attempt to get a better grasp of the "big picture," an overview of a life hereafter. The Bible states with clarity and certainty that each human being will have an eternal spiritual life after his or her mortal life ends. It states further that all of humankind will be divided into only two classes of people, those who are saved (believers) and those who are lost (unbelievers). These two classes of people are also referred to as Christians and non-Christians.

The Bible promises that believers will attain life in an everlasting home in a majestic and awesome place called Heaven. There, they will be in the glorious presence of God Almighty forever. On the other hand, the unsaved will be relegated to an eternal home in an equal but opposite place called Hell, a place of unthinkable anguish and torment. The lost will be separated from God forever, and they will be in the everlasting presence of the devil, or Satan. The Scriptures call this the second death. The Bible thus affirms that there are, or will be, real places called Heaven and Hell.

The Bible speaks of end-time judgments, or judgments at the end of this age. These judgments will take place subsequent to the Second Coming of Christ. Our final destinations of either Heaven or Hell, however, will not be determined by these end-time judgments. That determination will be made before we die physical deaths. Each of us can secure an eternal home in Heaven in God's glorious presence simply by believing in Jesus Christ, God's Son, and accepting Him as our personal Savior and Lord. Believing in Jesus means confessing our sins to God, repenting from our sinful ways, trusting in Jesus for our salvation, and committing our life to Jesus. But, if we reject Jesus Christ and do not believe in Him, we are doomed to eternity in Hell, separated from God forever. We have only two choices, either to accept Jesus or to reject Him.

The human mind cannot comprehend the glory and beauty of Heaven, nor can humankind fathom the terrible anguish and torment of Hell. The authors of the Bible, inspired by God's Holy Spirit, attempted to describe Heaven and Hell using the very best language at their disposal. However, words do not exist to adequately portray Heaven and Hell, and if they did, the human mind could not comprehend them. The Bible states that Heaven will be more glorious than human beings can imagine, and I believe also that the punishment of Hell will be far greater than the human intellect can understand. The very essence of Heaven is that believers will be in God's awesome presence forever. In a like manner, the very essence of Hell is that the unsaved will be separated from God forever.

Perhaps our most accurate perception of Heaven can be realized by comparing it to the Garden of Eden depicted in the Book of Genesis in the Bible. Adam and Eve enjoyed God's daily presence and fellowship, they were happy in a God-ordained husband and wife relationship, all their needs were provided for, they lived in a lush garden of unspeakable beauty, their work was pleasant and enjoyable, and they expected to live forever. Surely Heaven must be somewhat like the Garden of Eden where conditions were ideal.

Christ's second coming will usher in the end of this age, and time as we know it will end. The events that will occur after Christ returns are described primarily in the Book of Revelation. Our study has incorporated the author's interpretations of key passages in Revelation, but I believe the same basic conclusions would be reached if other valid interpretations were considered instead. The primary message of Revelation is that when Christ returns He will gather His saints and defeat Satan and his powers of evil. Ultimately, good will prevail over evil.

Looking Toward Eternity: A Life Hereafter?

Two significant judgments will take place after the Second Coming of Christ. The first, the Judgment Seat of Christ, will be for believers only. Each believer's deeds, or works, will be judged to determine what rewards he or she will obtain in Heaven. Good deeds will be judged along with the bad, and each believer's rewards will be according to the sum total of his or her deeds in the flesh. These rewards will include several crowns that will be bestowed on particular believers because of their special service for the Lord. For example, the Crown of Life will be given to those believers who have suffered unusual persecution and tribulations as the result of their faithfulness and their service for the Lord. Other crowns include the Crown of Glory, the Crown of Rejoicing, the Incorruptible Crown, and the Crown of Righteousness. The human mind cannot imagine the specific nature of these rewards and crowns in Heaven. We know only three things for certain about them. They will come from God, they will be good, and they will be very desirable for those residents of Heaven who receive them.

The second judgment will be for unbelievers only, the Great White Throne Judgment. It will be similar in nature but the direct opposite of the Judgment Seat of Christ for the saved. Each lost person's deeds in the flesh, both good and bad, will be judged at the Great White Throne Judgment to determine the degree of punishment he or she will experience in Hell. The human mind is also incapable of comprehending the exact nature of the torment and punishment in Hell. We know only three things for sure about that punishment. It will be allowed by God, it will be bad, and it will be extremely undesirable for the residents of Hell.

Contrary to what many people believe, Heaven will not be the same for all believers. Neither will Hell be the same for all of the unsaved. Because some of the saved in Heaven will receive rewards and crowns different from those received by other believers, Heaven will not be the same for them. We adopted the view in our analysis of this issue in chapter six that Christians will have varying capacities to enjoy the full majesty and glory of Heaven, depending on their deeds in the flesh. We concluded that a believer's deeds, or works, in this mortal life will be somewhat of a measure of how well that person will be able to enjoy the full splendor of Heaven. We referred to this as different degrees of Heaven. If Heaven were to be the same for all saved people, regardless of their works, then there would be no need for the Judgment Seat of Christ, and rewards and crowns in Heaven would be of no significance.

Each lost person's works, both good and bad, will be judged at the Great White Throne Judgment to determine the degree of punishment he or she will experience in Hell. We viewed this as the residents of Hell having varying capacities to tolerate the terrible anguish and torment of Hell. So, an unbeliever's works in the flesh will be somewhat of a measure of how well that person will be able to tolerate the horrors of Hell. We referred to this as different degrees of Hell.

The Bible promises a resurrection for both believers and unbelievers, and we concluded that this will be a bodily resurrection. Jesus was the first to be resurrected, after He had been dead and in the grave for three days. God raised Him from the grave, and then, Jesus appeared to several individuals, He appeared to His disciples as a group, and He appeared to over five hundred of His followers at one time. Jesus showed His nail-scarred hands and feet to His followers, He allowed them to touch Him, and He dined with them to affirm that He truly had a resurrected body. We do not know just how Jesus' resurrected body differs from our mortal bodies, but it has to be immortal and incorruptible. The Bible does tell us that Jesus could make Himself recognizable or unrecognizable at will and that He could appear or disappear at will. Through His resurrection, Jesus thus won victory over death and the grave.

Looking Toward Eternity: A Life Hereafter?

Jesus did much more than just rise from the dead Himself. By winning the victory over death and the grave, Jesus made it possible for Christians to be resurrected from the dead to a life eternal. His victory over death extends to all believers. The Bible teaches that the saved will receive resurrected bodies like that of our Lord Jesus. We too will receive immortal and incorruptible resurrected bodies. We surely cannot comprehend all that immortal and incorruptible body will encompass, but we know it will be perfect in every way.

The Scriptures also tell us when Christians will receive their resurrected bodies. At His second coming, Jesus will bring with Him the souls of believers that have died. At that time, those believers' souls will be united with their resurrected bodies in the air. Then, Christians still living will be transformed to receive their resurrected bodies, and they will meet Christ in the air. So, all saved people will receive their resurrected bodies at the end of this age when Christ returns, which will be at some unknown time in the future.

Non-Christians will also receive resurrected bodies, but the Bible seems to be unclear as to just how and when that will happen. However, it will be after the Second Coming of Christ and before the Great White Throne Judgment, wherein all the lost will be relegated to Hell. Unbelievers' souls will be united with their resurrected bodies, and they will be cast into Hell. This is referred to as the second death, and it will not be experienced by believers.

We know that Christians will reach their final destination of Heaven after Christ returns, which will be at the end of this age. We also know that the soul of a saved person will leave his or her body at the moment of physical death. The question then is "What happens to our souls between the times of our mortal deaths and the end of this age?" We concluded that our souls will leave our dead bodies and go to a place the Bible calls Paradise. It seems that Paradise is either Heaven, a part of Heaven, or a place somehow associated with Heaven. The souls of believers will remain in Paradise until Christ returns, and at that time they will be united with their resurrected bodies.

The Bible tells us that the unsaved will reach their final destination of Hell at some time after Christ returns. We also concluded that a lost person's soul will leave his or her body at the moment of death and then it will go to a place that is either Hell, a part of Hell, or somehow related to Hell. The Scriptures do not name this initial residence of an unbeliever's soul subsequent to his or her physical death, but it appears to be a place analogous to Paradise for Christians.

Believers will receive resurrected bodies at the Second Coming of Christ, and their souls will be united with their resurrected bodies. They will then go before the Judgment Seat of Christ to determine their rewards in Heaven. The saved will reign with Christ during the Thousand-Year Millennium, and then they will spend eternity in Heaven in the glorious presence of Almighty God.

Non-Christians will receive resurrected bodies at some time after Christ returns, and their souls will be united with their resurrected bodies. They will be subjected to the Great White Throne Judgment, wherein their deeds in the flesh will be judged to determine the degree of their punishment in Hell. They will then be cast into Hell, the second death, where they will be separated from God forever.

Chapter 11

OUR FINAL DESTINATION

We have delved into God's Word to find out what the Bible has to say about a life beyond this mortal life. We may disagree on many of the interpretations and conclusions presented in this book, but I believe most of us will agree on the one critical question that each of us must address. That is, "Where will I spend eternity?" I cannot answer that question for a single reader of this book, but I can answer for myself.

We have concluded that a person can get to Heaven only by believing in Jesus Christ and accepting Him as his or her personal Savior and Lord. One verse in Scripture sums it up.

> For God so loved the world, that he gave his only begotten Son, that whosoever believeth in him should not perish, but have everlasting life.
>
> —John 3:16 KJV

The key word in this verse is "believeth." What exactly does it mean? The New Testament was originally written in Greek, and the English language does not offer a word that adequately expresses the full meaning of the Greek word translated "believeth." The Greek word translated "believe" (or "believeth") incorporates an element of knowledge or belief, an element of trust, and an element of commitment. So, what do I actually mean when I say, "I believe in Jesus Christ"?

1. I believe Jesus Christ is God's Son, that I am a sinner separated from God and doomed to eternity in Hell, that I cannot save myself from that dreadful fate, that only Jesus can save me, and that He sacrificed His life on a cross at Calvary to pay for my sins.
2. I confess my sins to God and trust in Jesus Christ to forgive me and to save me from eternity in Hell.
3. I commit my life to Jesus Christ, allowing Him to be Lord of my life. What He wants me to be has a higher priority in my life than that of my personal desires.

What appears to be a simple word, "believe," has a much broader and deeper meaning when used in Scripture.

Salvation in Jesus Christ is not a matter of feeling or emotion; it is a willful decision involving trust and commitment. Let me hasten to add, though, that quite often there are emotions and feelings accompanying that decision. That certainly was true for me when I believed in Jesus and accepted Him as my Savior and Lord shortly before my fiftieth birthday. I can now confidently answer the question regarding my eternal home. I will spend eternity in Heaven in the glorious presence of my God.

But what about you, the reader? Will you spend eternity in Heaven or Hell? There is no other choice. I pray that each reader of this book will examine his or her relationship with God and then answer honestly the critical question concerning his or her final destination. If you have not already done so, I pray also that each of you will make that all-important decision to believe in

Our Final Destination

Jesus Christ and accept Him as your personal Savior and Lord. I hope and pray that I will see each of you in Heaven, and may God bless you in a mighty way in this mortal life.

To order additional copies of

LOOKING
TOWARD
ETERNITY

Have your credit card ready and call:

1-877-421-READ (7323)

or please visit our web site at
www.pleasantword.com

Also available at:
www.amazon.com
and
www.barnesandnoble.com
www.christianbook.com